The Householder's Electrical Guide

GEOFFREY BURDETT

THE HOUSEHOLDER'S ELECTRICAL GUIDE

STANLEY PAUL, LONDON

STANLEY PAUL & CO LTD
3 Fitzroy Square, London W1

AN IMPRINT OF THE HUTCHINSON GROUP

London Melbourne Sydney Auckland
Wellington Johannesburg Cape Town
and agencies throughout the world

First published 1973

*This book has been set in Imprint type, printed in Great Britain
on antique wove paper by Anchor Press, and
bound by Wm. Brendon, both of Tiptree, Essex*

ISBN 0 09 116791 4 (cased)
     0 09 116790 6 (paperback)

Contents

Acknowledgements

The author acknowledges with thanks the assistance given by John O'Mahoney, Lecturer in Charge of Electrical Installation Work at the Harrow College of Technology and Art, for his helpful suggestions, reading the manuscript and checking proofs.

Illustrations

Line Drawings

Photographs

Between pages 56 and 57
Consumer unit with fuses
Consumer unit with miniature circuit breakers
Rewirable fuse
Cartridge fuse
Miniature circuit breaker
Earth leakage circuit breaker
13A fused plug
Modern ceiling rose showing terminals and connections
Encased ceiling rose
Shaver supply unit
Fitting immersion heater into flange of hot water cylinder
Dual immersion heater
Side entry immersion heater

Between pages 120 and 121
Instantaneous water heater
Storage water heater
Extractor fan
Fuel effect radiant heater
Convector heater
Oil-filled radiator
Washing machine, front loader
Fan heater
Kettle
Food mixer

Preface

When it comes to home improvements more and more people are becoming 'do-it-yourself' orientated. For there is much personal satisfaction to be gained from fixing or building something yourself, apart from the obvious financial saving when no contractor's bills have to be met.

This book has been written to tell the practical householder and the mechanically minded housewife everything about the domestic electrical installation. No puzzling formulae have been used—for none are necessary. The work is entirely practical, ranging from replacing a blown fuse to installing an electric storage heater. And the emphasis is always on safety because all information given conforms strictly to the official wiring regulations.

There is a lot of other useful information too: about how to get the electricity supply put on when moving house; what tariff to choose; how to read a meter and how to instruct an electrical contractor, should one need to be called in for jobs outside the householder's capabilities.

Electrical work is slightly different to other jobs which the householder might undertake because it does involve a high standard of proficiency for it to be completely safe. This does not mean that the layman should be reluctant to, say, rewire his entire house. On the contrary, every householder should know as much as possible about the source of power and light with which he constantly lives, and be capable of altering or fixing it when it becomes necessary.

The young man entering the electrical contracting industry, the shop assistant who needs to answer many questions from customers and the young woman embarking on a career as an Electrical Housecraft Adviser will all find this book an up-to-date and comprehensive source of facts.

In writing *The Householder's Electrical Guide*, Geoffrey Burdett has drawn on many years' experience in the electricity supply and electrical contracting industries as a professional, and from answering many thousands of questions asked by his magazine readers over a period of nearly twenty years. It follows, therefore, that you will find an answer to most of your problems by consulting this book.

1 | The Home Electrical Installation

Before the sixteenth century it was known that certain substances under friction, such as amber, would produce enough energy or static electricity to attract lightweight objects. But it took another two hundred years of scientific research before this natural phenomenon was tapped successfully and generated for practical use. From the discovery in 1802 that an electric spark, when struck between two carbon electrodes, emitted a brilliant light—the arc lamp—we are now able to flick a switch and produce the same effect. Today the trend is towards 'all-electric' homes, and it only takes a power cut for us to realise just how much we depend on this silent force to provide our basic needs; to light our way, keep us warm, cook our food and motivate all those labour saving appliances which have become necessities in our lives.

To better understand domestic electrical applications we should first look at the source of power which, for the householder, is that mysterious and complicated set of wires, fuses and meters usually secreted beneath the stairs or in some equally dark and inaccessible place.

CONSUMER UNITS

The home electrical installation consists of a number of individual circuits of various current ratings which radiate from a centrally situated position, usually adjacent to the electricity board's meter and fuse box. In modern or modernised installations these circuits are distributed from a consumer unit containing the necessary main switch plus all the fuses. In older installations circuits are supplied from a number of main switch and fuse units of various types and current ratings. (These should be replaced by a modern consumer unit as soon as practicable.)

Fig. 1   Circuit wiring connections in a 6-way consumer unit

A house equipped with electric storage heating usually has a second consumer unit to supply these circuits. This is necessary because storage heating is time controlled to operate only during cheap night rate periods.

A consumer unit contains a number of fuses of different current ratings—one fuse for each circuit—and sometimes spare fuseways which are blanked off for future extensions to the installation. (When fitting a new unit at least one such fuseway should be included.) Old type switch and fuse units, and some older fuse boards, have two fuses for each circuit; one for the live pole and one for the neutral pole. It is now obligatory to have only one fuse per circuit (single-pole fusing) as double-pole fusing is potentially dangerous.

Consumer units are made in a wide range of sizes from 2-way (two fuseways) to 10-way (ten fuseways) which is the largest likely to be required for domestic use. There are also 1-way units consisting of a main switch and fuse unit in the one casing. Usually termed *switch-fuse units*, these have current rating of 5A to 30A and higher, and are used for supplying single circuits. One version can be fitted with a fuse unit of any of four current ratings from 5A to 30A.

Multi-way units are usually fitted with a mixed rating of fuses to suit all the different circuits of the home installation. The current rating of the double-pole main switch varies with the size of the unit: 2-way units usually have a 45A main switch, larger sizes a 60A main switch, and the largest of all have an 80A or a 100A main switch. The tendency now is towards higher ratings to meet increasing load demands.

Standard current ratings of consumer unit fuses are 5A, 15A, 20A and 30A. The recently introduced 45A fuse is used to supply electric cookers and Electricaire central storage heating units. Although these various fuses can be placed in any order in a consumer unit it is usual to fit those of highest rating next to the main switch and the lowest ones farthest away.

All the fuses are colour coded according to their current rating (Table 2) which makes it easier to select the correct fuse and also to locate the one which has 'blown'.

Some consumer units are fitted with miniature circuit breakers (mcb's) instead of fuses. These are superior and are described on pages 22 and 23.

FUSES

A fuse distribution board, popularly termed a *fuse board*, is a consumer unit without a main switch. It is normally installed in larger houses, especially those with a cellar where Electricity Board's apparatus and meters are situated.

The fuse board has to be controlled by a main switch and fuse unit which must be situated within reach of the Electricity Board's service fuse and meter. Therefore these are fitted in a place like the cellar away from the fuse board which is centrally positioned where it is more convenient to get at. The principal reason for this is to reduce the lengths of the various circuit cables. In the modern house, the Board's apparatus and meter is often installed in the garage along with the consumer unit. Being relatively small and compact these houses do not warrant a separate main switch and fuse board.

Older fuse boards usually have fuses of one rating which means that separate systems are required for lighting and power. However, the modern fuse board has fuses of mixed current rating and covers all circuits as does the consumer unit.

ELECTRICITY BOARD'S SERVICE FUSE AND METER

The supply of electricity comes into the house via a mains service cable run either underground or overhead, and its size is determined by the load demand of all appliances and lighting. The cable terminates in a sealed *terminal box* containing the *service fuse* which is rated at 60A, 80A or 100A according to the assumed current demand of the installation. The terminal box normally contains only one fuse which is in the 'live' line or phase. Being the largest fuse of the installation it is least likely to blow in the event of a fault or excessive overload. Should this occur however it is necessary to send for the Electricity Board because only their engineers may break the seals to replace a fuse.

The Board's distribution system consists of three lines or phases colour coded red, yellow and blue plus the neutral. Houses are supplied from any one of the three phases and the colour is usually indicated by a disc on the apparatus. A house which takes above average load may be supplied from more than one phase and the terminal box then contains one fuse for each to effect a load balance.

However, as the voltage between phases is 415V, special measures are taken to ensure that only 240V is available in any one area of the house. This is clearly marked on the apparatus to avoid mistakes by the householder or his contractor.

2 | The Fuse

Of all electrical components the fuse is perhaps the most simple to understand and fix when necessary. Yet witness the 'blowing' of a fuse in some households and the ensuing pandemonium is quite surprising.

The purpose of a fuse is to protect appliances and cables from damage in the event of a fault; to isolate metalwork which would be charged with electricity at mains voltage and cause a serious shock; and to reduce the risk of fire arising from a fault or a seriously overloaded cable. It operates similarly to an intentional weak link in a chain and is often compared with a safety valve in a boiler system.

Every circuit has a fuse and in the modern installation most plugs have them too to protect individual appliances. Each uses a different current rating which is lower than that of the cable it is intended to protect (including flexible cords). When a fuse blows it indicates something is wrong, caused either by overloading or because of a fault in the wiring or in the appliance. When it is the plug fuse which blows the cause is almost always a fault because most appliances have a fixed loading which cannot be exceeded.

WHAT IT IS

Every fuse in a consumer unit, fuse board or switch/fuse unit has three principal components:

 (i) a fuse element—wire or cartridge
 (ii) fuse holder
 (iii) a fuse base or shield.

The fuse wire or cartridge is housed in the fuse holder which is plugged into the fuse base containing the contacts connected to the circuit cables.

TYPES

There are two principal types of circuit fuses used in the home installation

(i) re-wirable or semi-enclosed

(ii) cartridge fuses.

Both have similar and sometimes identical bases and a similar holder. The fuse wire of the rewirable type is partially enclosed in an asbestos tube and secured to the contacts by milled nuts or screws; the cartridge fuse is either secured by a plastic or metal clamp or is contained in a tightly fitting plastic tube which forms part of the fuse holder moulding. Of the two the cartridge fuse is superior but it has disadvantages. The majority of fuses used in the home are of the rewirable type which use fuse wire of tinned copper. Sizes and ratings are given in Table 1.

Rewirable fuses

Advantages : Easy and cheap to replace it is only necessary to have a card of the various wire ratings at hand to mend a fuse when it blows. A blown fuse can readily be seen by physical inspection when the fuse holder is withdrawn from the consumer unit.

Disadvantages : (i) Fuse wire deteriorates in use especially when the current in the circuit exceeds that of the fuse rating. The wire then runs hot which erodes the coating of tin and copper causing further overheating with the result that the fuse blows suddenly for no apparent reason (although a fault is suspected).

(ii) It is easily and therefore frequently abused. Larger fuse wire than necessary is inserted in the fuse holder in order to increase the load on the circuit or in an attempt to prevent a fuse blowing when there is a fault. The result is that the circuit cable becomes overloaded and is a potential fire risk. Hair pins and other objects which are sometimes used are an even greater hazard.

Fuses are sometimes uprated inadvertently because the householder is unaware of the correct rating but colour coding has been introduced to reduce the incidence of this. (Smaller fuse wire than the rating is also potentially dangerous because it runs hot under otherwise normal conditions.)

(iii) A rewirable fuse takes twice the current of the fuse wire rating to blow it. For example 60 amps is needed to blow a 30-amp fuse.

Cartridge fuses

A cartridge fuse consists of a special wire element contained in a cartridge filled with quartz particles (sand) or other mineral to quench the arc when the fuse blows. The ends of the element are secured to metal end caps which make the electrical contact with the fuse holder.

Advantages : (i) a blown fuse is easily replaced by a new one of the same current rating.

(ii) The physical size of the cartridge varies with the current rating of the fuse; the higher the current rating the larger the cartridge. It is therefore impossible to fit a 20A fuse, or a 30A fuse into a 5A fuse holder, either intentionally or by mistake.

(iii) Less excess current is needed to blow a cartridge fuse than a rewirable fuse and it therefore affords greater protection to the circuit. The current required to blow a cartridge fuse is about $1\frac{1}{2}$ times the current rating. For example, it needs 45 amps to blow a 30 amp fuse compared to 60 amps for a rewirable type.

Disadvantages : (i) Replacement costs are high especially when a fuse blows repeatedly because the fault has not been located.

(ii) Spare fuses of each rating have to be kept at hand.

(iii) Where no spare fuse is available there is a temptation to use fuse wire or some metallic object as a substitute. This is a dangerous practice for such fuses can disintegrate on blowing and cause substantial damage.

(iv) It is not possible by visual inspection to tell when a cartridge fuse has blown.

Plug fuses

These are cartridge fuses of the same high standard as circuit fuses.

B

FUSE RATINGS AND COLOURS

Cartridge fuse ratings are distinguished by their colour and also by the current rating stamped on them. Those which are also stamped BS.1361 have the following colours: 5A white; 15A blue; 20A yellow; 30A red and 45A green; spots of the same colour appear on the face of the holders. Holders of rewirable fuses are similarly coded. Plastic fuse holders are coloured, and plug fuses are coded; 3A blue (or red); 13A brown; all other ratings: black.

WHAT TO DO WHEN A FUSE BLOWS

When a circuit fuse blows extinguishing the lights in part of the house, you should be able to go into the meter cupboard and, with the aid of a torch, open the consumer unit cover and read on the inside which fuse supplies that circuit. If you have not listed the circuits you will have to withdraw each fuse until you find the one which has blown. If the lighting circuit has failed try the 5 amp fuses with their white colour coding. Examine each fuse in turn until you come to one with broken wire (though if a short circuit is the cause the wire will have disintegrated). If it is a cartridge fuse, first check that you have a spare. If necessary test it for it may be a dud. As you withdraw each fuse close the lid of the consumer unit and turn on the main switch to check if you have located the right circuit.

Having found it, you should first try to ascertain what caused the fuse to blow. If this happened immediately you switched on one of the lights and was accompanied by a slight bang or loud 'plop' it is probably a faulty flex. In either case you should turn off the switch and remove the bulb. If the fuse blew without anything being switched on at that moment and there was no 'plop' it is probably caused by fuse wire deterioration to which reference has already been made.

An iron, kettle or drill plugged into a light socket will also cause a fuse to blow. So will a heat/light unit. A ring circuit fuse will blow only through very serious overloading or because of a fault in the wiring: faulty appliances blow the individual plug fuse, not the circuit fuse.

Having located the fault you can now deal with the fuse. First you should turn off the main switch, not because it is dangerous to replace a fuse with the mains on but should there be a fault in the circuit the ensuing 'bang' when the new fuse is inserted will be less frightening.

Successive blowing of a fuse indicates a serious fault, probably in the wiring, which will need the service of an electrician. Recall whether you have recently driven nails in floorboards or drilled a wall which may have pierced a cable.

MENDING FUSES

The sequence for repairing a fuse is as follows

Rewirable fuse

Locate 'blown' fuse and remove from consumer unit of fuse board.

Try and locate the fault.

Remove old fuse wire from the fuse holder.

Insert new fuse wire of correct current rating in the porcelain of the fuse holder. Tighten screws and trim ends of wire but be careful not to stretch the wire too tightly when tightening the second screw.

Replace fuse holder in fuseway, switch on to test the circuit.

Cartridge fuse

Locate blown fuse, remove holder from consumer unit.

Try and locate fault.

Remove cartridge from fuse holder.

Check that fuse has blown and discard cartridge.

Insert new cartridge of correct current rating into fuse holder.

Replace fuse holder in fuseway of consumer unit, switch on to test the circuit.

Plug fuses

Remove cap of plug.

Prize out old fuse and discard it.

Select new fuse of appropriate current rating, first checking that the existing fuse was correct: 3A blue (or red) for appliances up to 700W including table lamps and floor standards: 13A brown for appliances between 700W and 3000W.

Insert the fuse in the plug, check that it is secure and makes good electrical contact.

Replace plug cap and test in socket.

Fused connection units

These, also termed *fused spur boxes*, contain a fuse identical in size and current ratings to that of plug fuses. It is removed by prizing out the anchored fuse holder on the front of the unit which allows the fuse to fall out. With some types the fuse holder is detachable and is removed by releasing a screw.

Fit in the new fuse and replace the cover using the reverse sequence.

TABLE 1

Rewirable Fuses

Current rating of fuse	Nominal diameter of wire	Circuit
amps	mm	
5	0·20	Lighting
15	0·50	Immersion heater
20	0·60	Radial including storage heaters
30	0·85	Ring circuit and 30A radial
45	1·25	Cooker

TABLE 2

Colour coding of cartridge circuit fuses

Cartridge colour	Current rating
	Amps
White	5
Blue	15
Yellow	20
Red	30
Green	45

3 | Miniature Circuit Breakers

A miniature circuit breaker (mcb) is a single-pole switch which automatically switches itself off when excess current flows through its operating coil and therefore in a circuit. It is a vastly superior alternative to a fuse and its only significant disadvantage is its higher initial cost but time and money otherwise spent in replacing fuses can be saved.

Current ratings are the same as for circuit fuses plus a number of intermediate ratings. For example at the lower end of the scale there is a $2\frac{1}{2}$A rating; at the upper end a 60A rating. Consumer units and fuse boards are made which will take either fuses or mcb's, but in the main consumer units are designed specifically for one or the other. In common with fuse-type consumer units, mcb's of the various current ratings are interchangeable enabling any mixture of ratings to be assembled to suit the installation.

The principal advantage of the mcb from the safety aspect is that it will 'trip' or switch off when current in excess of $1\frac{1}{4}$ times its rating flows in the circuit. Therefore a 30A mcb can be expected to trip when the current reached $37\frac{1}{2}$ amps compared to 45 amps for the cartridge fuse and 60 amps for the rewirable fuse. A lighting circuit normally protected by a 5A fuse must carry 10 amps before the fuse can be expected to blow. If instead an mcb is used in the consumer unit and the rating chosen is $2\frac{1}{2}$ amps the fault or overload current required to trip it will then be a little over 3 amps.

In addition to being automatic an mcb has a manually operated switch dolly which enables a circuit to be switched on and off without affecting other circuits. With some models this is a 3-position switch. In addition to 'Up' and 'Down' the switch dolly has a mid-way position which it returns to when tripped by a circuit fault or overload. This enables the householder to see at a glance whether the switch has been turned off manually or has tripped out because of a fault.

One make of mcb uses press-buttons instead of a switch. These are plug-in types fitted in the Wylex range of consumer units and fuse boards, and they are interchangeable with fuses—either rewirable or cartridge—and can be fitted to an existing unit by removing the fuse. A section of the consumer unit cover has also to be 'knocked-out' to accommodate the mcb's and to give access to manual switching. Circuit details are written on a label on the face of the mcb, the press-button gives the current rating and the units are colour-coded as for circuit fuses.

It is important to say at this stage that an mcb must not be confused with an elcb (earth leakage circuit breaker). An mcb is an excess-current device which is alternative to a fuse. An elcb, as is shown later is a substitute for an effective earthing arrangement and does not usually provide any excess current protection. Some patterns of elcb, however, incorporate overload protection.

4 | Earthing

The principal purpose of earthing in an installation is to ensure that the fuse will blow when a live wire comes into contact with conductible materials such as the metalwork casing of a heater, cooker, iron or kettle. That is why these appliances are fitted with three-core flex with the earth core secured to a terminal on the metalwork.

If an earthing system is ineffective or non-existent and a live wire comes into contact with the metal body of the appliance, the metalwork becomes charged with electricity at mains voltage but the fuse does not blow to cut off the current. The extent of shock received by a person touching the live framework depends on whether he is in contact with earthed metal and therefore providing an alternative path to earth. That is why an electric current can be dangerous to a person sitting in a bath of water where he is virtually enclosed in a conductible substance.

Fig. 2   Current flow through a person in contact with electricity

2-core flex

metal clad electrical appliance

bath

water pipe

fault to metal

'hand to hand shock'

Fig. 3   Current flow through a person in contact with electricity

For earthing to be effective it must be continuous from the appliance down through its flex, through the plug and socket, along the earth wire in a circuit cable, out of the house and through the ground to the Electricity Board's sub-station which might be a mile or so away. In the house the installation's earthing system terminates at an *electrode*. From there it can take any one of a variety of routes or earth paths, the most common being via the mains water pipes which are metal and therefore a good conductor for the earth fault current. With this method it is essential for the earthing lead to be well secured to the waterpipe on the street side of the stop cock where the mains pipe enters the house, therefore making a sound electrical and mechanical connection which is not subjected to corrosion.

However, since the introduction of plastic water pipes and insulated joints in metal pipes this can no longer be regarded as a reliable earthing method. Because of this unreliability, the regulations state that a water pipe must not be the sole means of earthing an installation. The principal alternative is now the metal sheath of the Electricity Board's cable which will carry the earth fault current direct to the sub-station. Then the Board provides an earthing terminal to which the installation earthing lead is connected. If cables are overhead and not metal sheathed the Board can sometimes use other methods to provide the necessary earth terminal. Where the Board cannot do this the householder has to provide an earth leakage circuit breaker which is used in conjunction with an earth rod electrode driven into the garden soil (see elcb's). An existing mains water pipe may continue to be used until the water authority substitutes plastic pipes. The Board advises the householder of such a change and either provides earthing facilities or tells the householder he must fit an elcb.

HOW EARTHING BLOWS THE FUSE

To understand how an effective earthing system works it is necessary to know a little bit more about the electricity supply system itself.

Of the two cables which come into the house—the live and the neutral—the neutral conductor is itself solidly connected to earth at the sub-station. This is often termed an *earthed neutral*. Therefore as well as having a voltage of 240V between the two poles, live and neutral, there is also a voltage of 240V between the live pole and earth but zero voltage between neutral and earth. The

Fig. 4   Normal current flow in circuit which has no fault

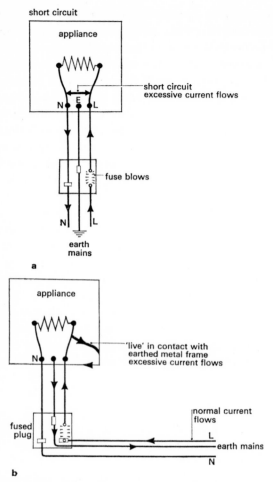

Fig. 5 Why a plug fuse blows (a) short circuit in appliance (b) live
conductor in contact with earthed metal frame of appliance

earthing system is therefore in effect an alternative return path
for the circuit current—but only under fault conditions.

Under normal conditions when, say, an electric fire is switched
on the current from the supply system enters the house via the live
conductor, passes through the 60A service fuse, through the meter

to the consumer unit, through the 30A ring circuit fuse, along the circuit cable to the socket and plug with its 13A fuse to the electric fire. From the fire the current returns via the neutral conductor and eventually reaches the sub-station but without passing through any more fuses as they are all in the live pole of the system. The amount of current is determined solely by what the heater demands which if it is a 1-bar fire is about 5 amps. The element has acted as a resistance or current limiter. Switch on instead a 2-bar fire and the current in the circuit will be double that of one.

If the insulation of the live flex becomes damaged through heat, and the now bared conductor touches the earthed metal frame of the fire, electric current immediately flows through the earthing system and back to the sub-station. As this current would by-pass the heater there would be no elements or other resistance to limit it. In effect it would be a short circuit. This heavy current which always arises from short circuits would flow through the live conductor from the power source in the usual way. In so doing it would pass through three fuses in the house: the 60–100A service fuse, the 30A circuit fuse and the 13A plug fuse. Being the lowest current rating of the three the plug fuse would be the one to go. This fuse would itself limit the fault current to about 25 amps which is the fusing current of a 13A plug fuse. If there is no fused plug the circuit fuse would blow. As a 30A fuse requires up to 60 amps to blow it the circuit would have to take this strain which might damage the electric fire, and cause the rubber insulated flex to ignite. That is why plug fuses are so important in safeguarding against fires from electrical faults in the house.

If, however, the householder had omitted to connect the earth core of the flex to the plug or the earth core had come adrift in the heater there would be no continuous path for the fault current and the fuse would not blow. Instead the metal frame of the fire would remain live at the mains voltage and be a shock risk for all who came in contact with it. In fact if the earthing system is broken at any point the fuse could not blow, and it is therefore essential for all joints to be properly made and any earthing clips and connections well secured and occasionally inspected for corrosion.

For obvious reasons gas pipes, hot water pipes and the secondary cold water pipes supplying taps from the storage system must not be used for earthing. Where there is a likelihood that electric cables come into contact with such pipes it is necessary to earth exposed metalwork such as hot water radiators, the hot water storage tank and even the bath and its waste pipe. Some modern baths (made to BS) have an earth terminal for this purpose. The earthing of extraneous metalwork is termed *bonding*. Green pvc insulated cable is used for this and the connection to earth is made at the earth terminal within or near the main consumer unit. In addition it is now necessary to bond, or cross-bond the gas and cold water mains services. To do this a bonding clamp is fitted to the mains water pipe on the street side of the stopcock where the pipe enters the house, and to the gasmains pipe on the house side of the gas meter. Green pvc insulated cable connected to the installation earth terminal is used for this cross-bonding of services.

5 | Earth Leakage Circuit Breakers

An earth leakage circuit breaker (elcb) is a main switch automatically operated by an earth fault current flowing in a circuit. The essential feature for its operation is a tripping coil which, when energised either directly or indirectly, releases a latching device which allows the circuit breaker to open and cut off the current to the faulty circuit. In this respect the elcb functions similarly to a fuse but only for earth fault currents. It will not operate when a short circuit occurs across live and neutral poles or when the circuit is overloaded. For those faults a fuse is still needed.

An important characteristic of the elcb is that only a small earth current is needed to operate it. That is why it is used mainly where the water authority or the Electricity Board are unable to supply the householder with earthing facilities.

An earth rod electrode driven into the garden soil cannot be used on its own because it is unable to provide an earth path to the sub-station of sufficient low impedence for earth fault currents up to and in excess of 60 amps. It must therefore be used in conjunction with an elcb, needing only a small earth fault current to operate it.

There are two principal types of elcb used in the home installation: current-operated and voltage-operated. The first choice should be the current-operated type although this is the more expensive of the two. Made by a number of firms the current-operated type has two current ratings: one is its rating as a main switch which can be up to 100 amps and the other is its operating current, usually either ½A or 1A (the 1A size is the more common). This means that the earthing system including the rod electrode will need to handle about 1 amp of earth fault current. Where soil resistance is such that neither 1A nor $\frac{1}{2}$A can be handled by the earth loop system it becomes necessary to install a voltage-operated elcb. This needs very little current to operate the trip coil and it can be used when the resistance of the earth loop is many hundreds of ohms.

The operation and wiring of the two types differ considerably. The current-operated type has what is termed a *core balanced transformer*. Under normal conditions a balance is maintained but when an earth fault current flows in a circuit this balance is upset causing the trip coil to be energised which trips the circuit breaker. The earthing lead of the installation goes direct to the earth rod electrode and is not connected at all to the earthing system. See diagram 6.

Fig. 6   Connection between circuit breaker and installation

With the voltage-operated type the earth fault current from the installation to the earth rod passes through the trip coil, the connections being made at the F and E terminals of the elcb. However, there are a number of inherent disadvantages which can affect its correct operation when a fault occurs, mainly that the fault current which takes a path of least resistance may find an alternative route to earth such as via the water system, which will therefore deprive the circuit breaker of sufficient voltage to operate the trip coil. For this reason the earth electrode must be kept well clear of any other electrode including the mains water pipe in the garden. Also two or more voltage-operated elcb's should not be used in the same installation without special measures being taken. When the Electricity Board stipulates this kind of elcb allowances have to be made for these characteristics, i.e. the earthing rod should be at least 4 ft long and preferably copper-coated steel.

ELCB'S AS LIFE SAVERS

The ordinary elcb, current- or voltage-operated, will not protect a person from a fatal shock if he touches a live wire any more than a fuse will. But recent development, a high-sensitivity current-operated elcb, does give this protection for it requires only about 25–30 milliamps to operate it at a speed of under 20 milliseconds. An extremely low current of such short duration can be withstood by the human body but a current slightly higher than this will paralyse the muscles and prevent the victim from 'letting go' of the live contact. The extended duration of the current which passes through the body then results in death.

Because of its high sensitivity this type of elcb has limited application and it is only used for protecting individual circuits and appliances rather than complete installations. It is particularly suitable for protecting circuits supplying power tools, electrically operated hedge trimmers and mowers where the risk of shock is high and 'nuisance tripping' caused by slight moisture does not matter. It is not so appropriate for refrigerators or automatic cookers where 'nuisance tripping' could be inconvenient. A useful model for the householder which requires no alterations to the fixed wiring is the Pluguard; a portable high sensitivity elcb which plugs into a 13A or 15A socket-outlet and contains a socket-outlet for the appliance plug.

It is important to stress that elcb's only provide protection if a live conductor is touched when standing on, or in contact with, the ground or earthed metal. It does not prevent a fatal shock if both live and neutral conductors are touched when standing on an insulated surface. *Nothing can prevent a fatal shock in those circumstances.*

6 | Flexible Cords

A flexible cord is an electric cable with either one, two or three insulated conductors known as *cores*, each consisting of numerous strands. The small flex used in the home installation has 16-strand conductors; the largest has conductors of 65 strands. It is these strands which provide the cable's necessary flexibility.

Most flexible cords have an overall insulated sheathing to provide extra mechanical protection to the insulated cores but some twin-core flex as well as single-core flex is non-sheathed.

Six types or classes of flexible cords are used in the homes depending on the application and the situation. These are:

(i) *Twisted, twin non-sheathed flex insulated with rubber or pvc* used for pendant lighting fittings and for appliances where the cord is not subject to abrasion. Rubber insulated flex has silk or cotton covered cores in various colours to match the situation. The pvc insulation of some flex is transparent but may only be used for pendant lighting where the flex is open to view.

(ii) *Parallel-twin non-sheathed pvc insulated flex* used for light fittings. This may also be fitted to appliances such as electric clocks and other small stationary equipment where the cord is not subject to abrasion and undue flexing.

(iii) *Braided circular flex* made in both 2-core and 3-core versions and has a 2-colour braiding. Cotton fillers provide the circular cross-section. It is fitted to a wide variety of domestic electrical appliances including portable electric fires but is confined to dry situations indoors. Cores are usually rubber insulated.

(iv) *Unkinkable flex* 3-core rubber insulated flex has a light rubber sheathing in which is partially embedded a 2-colour braid. It is fitted to electric irons and kettles.

(v) *Circular sheathed flex* is made in 2-core and 3-core versions with either a rubber or pvc sheath. This is a general purpose

c

flexible cord for inside and outside use and is fitted to vacuum cleaners, floor polishers, electric drills and a variety of portable electric tools where a long lead is required. Extension flexible cords, often contained on drums fitted with a socket-outlet, are of this type too. Sheath colours are grey or black for general purpose use, bright orange or yellow for hedge trimmers, mowers and other gardening tools, and white (but sometimes black) for pendant light fittings when it is used instead of twisted twin flex. When cable is used from a drum always unroll the cable from the drum or it may overheat. Heat resistant circular flex insulated in butyl rubber of various compounds is made for connection to immersion heaters and other heaters where there is high temperature within the terminal box.

(vi) *Flat twin sheathed flex* is a version of parallel twin flex with pvc insulation and sheathing. It is fitted to some double-insulated, and all-insulated appliances where sheathing is necessary to prevent the abrasion of the core insulation, and colour coding of the cores is desirable.

CORE COLOURS

Since 1970 it has been a statutory requirement that every portable domestic electrical appliance and every earthed light fitting be wired with 3-core flex of standard colours. A shop selling either new or second-hand appliances and fittings with flex in any other colours is comitting an offence.

The new colours are: *brown* (live); *blue* (neutral); and striped *green/yellow* (earth). These replace the former flex core colours which were standard in Britain: red (live); black (neutral); and green (earth). Flexible cords in other countries had cores of various colours but these are now the same as those here.

The statutory requirement does not extend to 2-core flex for this is only fitted to appliances and light fittings which do not require an earth connection. Nevertheless, two-core sheathed flex is now made with the new core colours of brown for the 'live' core and blue for the neutral. The cores of pvc twisted twin and parallel twin flex are one colour or transparent. One core is sometimes distinguished by ribbing along its length but as this is not always so and this type of flex cannot be used where the lamp or appliance is controlled by a single-pole cord switch or built-in switch or a thermostat, which must be connected to the live pole.

FLEX SIZES

Flexible cord used in the home is made in a number of sizes having a range of current ratings from 3A to 25A. The number and diameter of strands differ with the current rating. All are in metric sizes as shown in Table 3.

RENEWING A FLEX

When renewing a flexible cord on an appliance it will almost certainly be fitted with the old type flex. As the new flex will be in the new colour coding it is important to remember both the old and the new colours so that you connect it correctly. If it is an imported appliance and the flex cores are entirely different colours to those in Britain, make sure you know which are the different terminals and do not hesitate to have the appliance checked at the shop where you buy the new flex.

EXTENDING FLEX

A flexible cord must not be lengthened by twisting the ends and wrapping the joint in insulation tape. Any joint must be mechanically strong as well as electrically sound and this is only possible when a proper flex connector is used. Generally, it is better to discard the flex and fit a new length. The exception is a power tool lead or other long circular sheathed flex for which extension leads are available, as an alternative.

There are two types of connector: One is solid with fixed terminals and cord grips for anchoring the sheath. The conductors of the old and new flex must be of the correct polarity, which means they must be fitted into the correct terminals. The rule is: brown to red; blue to black; and green/yellow to green. Where both the existing and the extension flex are of the new colours cores of identical colours are, of course, inserted in the terminals.

The other type of connector is a two-piece 'plug-and-socket' unit. The terminals are marked *L N* and *E* in each section so there should be no problem. It is, however, essential for the plug portion of this connector to be fitted to the appliance side of the flex extension and for the socket portion to be connected to the mains side which is 'live' when the lead is plugged into the supply in the house socket-outlet. The socket (or female portion) is usually marked *MAINS* to avoid a wrong connection.

CONNECTING FLEX TO A PLUG

A flexible cord must be connected correctly as shown in the photographs for the standard 13A fused plug. The green/yellow (or green) earth core is the most important from the safety aspect and should be connected first to the large pin in the centre top. The brown (or red) which is the live and next important is connected to the terminal on the right and in contact with the fuse. The blue (or black) core, the neutral, is connected to the terminal on the left. Before fitting the plug cover ensure that the flex sheath is well anchored in the sheath clamp so that there is no undue strain on the conductors when the flex is pulled.

Plugs of other sizes and types have various terminal arrangements and anchorage and should be carefully examined before renewing the flex.

PLUG ADAPTORS

Plug adaptors are multi-outlet devices which enable more than one appliance to be run off a single socket-outlet. They should be used only where absolutely necessary to avoid numerous trailing flexes and the risk of overloading a socket.

Where plugs smaller than the main plug are used the adaptor should contain a fuse to protect the flex of lower current rating. *Some mixed rating adaptors do not have fuses and these can be potentially dangerous.*

SOCKET DISTRIBUTION UNITS

These are a form of adaptor but connected by flexible cord to a parent plug. The total loading on the unit must not exceed the rated capacity of the socket supplying it. Some distribution units contain a circuit breaker to prevent overloading and most have neon indicators. The units are particularly suitable for supplying small tools and portable lamps in the workshop and garage, and they have some use in the house but they should not be regarded as a substitute for additional, permanently wired socket-outlets. Single sockets for connection to an extension lead are termed *trailing sockets* and are of rubber or pvc construction.

TABLE 3

Flexible Cords

Size	Current rating	Maximum weight supportable by twin flex	Application
mm²	amps	kg (lb)	
0·5	3	2 (3)	Lighting fittings
0·75	6	3 (5)	Lighting fittings and small appliances
1·0	10	5 (10)	Appliances up to 2400 watts
1·5	15	5 (10)	Appliances up to 3600 watts
2·5	20	5 (10)	Appliance up to 4800 watts
4	25	5 (10)	Appliances up to 6000 watts

7 | Lamps and Lighting

The most commonly used electric lamp in the home is the ordinary light bulb. This has a tungsten wire filament enclosed in a gas-filled glass bulb and a brass bayonet (bc) lamp cap. The bulb is made in two principal forms: single-coil filament and coiled coil filament which gives the greater light output for a given wattage.

Fig. 7   Cut-away view of light bulb

The single-coil bulb is made in a dozen sizes from 15W to 1500W. The coiled coil is made in five sizes: 40W, 60W, 100W, 150W and 300W. But the principal sizes used in the home are: 40W, 60W, and 100W. Since coiled coil lamps are more efficient and give more light than single coil they should be chosen in the available sizes (wattage).

Another relevant variation is the glass bulb or envelope itself. This can be plain, or pearl; bulb or mushroom shaped. Mushroom shape bulbs all have coiled coil filaments. Pink pearl is another variant, these being mainly single-coil lamps but some are mushroom shaped.

Pearl and pink pearl bulbs are used mainly in pendants and fittings where the lamp is exposed to the eyes. Clear bulbs which are slightly more efficient are preferred in enclosed and in decorative fittings. Bulbs in different colours are also available and there are a number of special lamps of various shapes (such as 'Gala') used in fittings without shades. For wall lighting and some pendants, candle lamps can be used which come in a range of shapes: olive plain, olive twisted, in clear, opal and pink pearl and frosted coloured and small round bulbs of 15W and 20W. One candle bulb even incorporates a flickering wick.

STRIP LIGHTS

Strip type lamps 9–12 in. (225–300 mm) long have a tungsten filament enclosed in a clear or frosted tubular glass envelope with single-contact bc lamp caps at each end. They come in 30W and 60W sizes, in white, frosted pink and amber colours and have numerous purposes in the home from picture lighting to illuminating the aquarium.

A more attractive version is the architectural tubular lamp which can be either straight, in lengths from 12–48 in. (300–1200 mm) of 35–150 watts, or curved at 60 watts. All are opal, have single-pin caps for fitting into special lampholders and are fixed direct to the wall or ceiling.

LONGER-LIFE ELECTRIC LIGHT BULBS

The ordinary electric light bulb has an average life of about 1000 light hours. This is comparatively short because the bulbs are designed to produce the highest possible light output for a given wattage. It is possible to produce bulbs with a much longer life but only at the expense of light output. Such bulbs are now available some of which have double the life of the ordinary bulb and others have an almost indefinite life.

They cost more to buy but are worth trying out especially in fittings where you do not want to be replacing bulbs at fairly short intervals.

FLUORESCENT LIGHTING

A fluorescent lamp is an electronic tube in various lengths and wattages, operated only in conjunction with ballast gear which is usually a choke plus a starter switch and capacitors. Some, termed quick-start or instant start, have no starter switch and some use a special filament lamp as a ballast.

The normally preferred type is the switch start for these last longer, but where starting delay causes annoyance the quick-start switchless type is better. The advantage of the lamp ballast type is that the fitting is noiseless; there is no characteristic hum from the choke. The disadvantage is that they consume more current although the light they emit can be usefully employed.

HOW A FLUORESCENT TUBE OPERATES

The tubular glass envelope is coated on the inside with a fluorescent powder and contains a small quantity of special gas. At each end is a cathode or electrode consisting of a wire filament or braided element which is connected to a bi-pin or bc lamp cap.

When the lamp is switched on a high-voltage current produced by the choke 'strikes' across the two cathodes and starts a flow of electrons along the tube. These electrons bombard the glass envelope, excite the fluorescent coating and produce the characteristic light. (Various tones or colours are obtained by mixing impurities with the fluorescent powder.)

The starter switch is a small 'make and break' device which is made in two types. One, the thermal type, may include a small heater element similar to a thermostat enclosed in a metal canister which has four contact pins for fitting into a starter holder on the fitting. The other is the glow type with only two pins and no heater element, and is the usual domestic fitting.

There is no pre-warming in the quick-start circuit for there is no starter switch. The result is that some of the cathodes' coating is eroded each time the tube is switched on, so reducing the expected life of the lamp. Some such erosion occurs with switch start circuits too but it is much less. Since, however, the expected life of a fluorescent tube is up to 7000 light hours (representing about ten years) a slightly shorter life can hardly be termed a financial problem. Nevertheless it is an economy to minimise the switch on and off frequency and therefore reduce the rate of erosion. Fluorescent lights should therefore be used where lighting is required for a continuous period. For example, in a kitchen, where it is usually installed, it is better to have a filament lamp for the general lighting controlled by the switch at the door and a fluorescent tube where extra light is needed operated by a local switch. The tube can be positioned over the sink or working area and its switch can be cord-operated from the ceiling.

Quick-start fluorescent tubes usually have a narrow metal stripe running throughout their length in contact with each lamp cap. This is an earthing stripe and is connected to the earthing system and to an earth terminal on the lampholders and to the metalwork of the fitting. This assists in starting the lamp and without it the tube is unlikely to light or 'strike'. With some the tube must be fitted to within an inch of the earthed metalwork, usually the reflector of the fitting. When buying and fixing a fluorescent fitting of the quick-start type it is essential to ensure that there is an earth conductor at the lighting point or that one is installed. It is also important to remember that a switch start tube will not operate in a quick-start fitting but a quick-start tube will operate in either. Shops sell only the more popular sizes of quick-start tubes which are purchased for either type of circuit or fitting and there is no need to ask specifically for either.

Faults and their remedies concerning fluorescent tubes and fittings are detailed on page 46.

CHOOSING THE TUBE COLOUR

Among the numerous tones or colours produced by fluorescent tubes are 'Daylight', 'Warmwhite', 'De-Luxe Warmwhite', 'Natural' and various proprietory names such as 'Softone', 'Kolor-rite' and many more.

The 'colour' must be suitable for the home and most widely used is De Luxe Warmwhite which can be used in most fittings. Proprietory colours such as 'Softone' are also suitable for the home and are sold for that purpose in addition to other applications where a warm light is required.

The principal advantage of fluorescent lighting is that it gives much more light than does the tungsten filament bulb of the same wattage.

For example: a 40W De-Luxe Warmwhite tube produces about 2000 lumens of light compared with under 400 lumens from a 40W coiled coil filament lamp. As, however, the choke of a fluorescent fitting also consumes electricity, allowance must be made for this when making current consumption comparisons.

A more realistic comparison is a 40W fluorescent Warmwhite tube which produces 2000 lumens and a 60W coiled coil bulb which produces 660 lumens. On that basis, allowing 20 watts for the choke, it can be said that a De-Luxe Warmwhite fluorescent tube provides three times the light of a tungsten filament lamp for the same electricity consumption. White, Warmwhite, Daylight and Natural colour tubes all have a greater light output than De-Luxe Warmwhite, other 'colours' produce less light, the lowest being Artificial Daylight with its 1200 lumens for a 40W tube.

SIZES AND TYPES OF TUBES

Among the extensive range of fluorescent tubes there are three principal sizes most suitable for the home: the 5 ft (150 mm), 65W, the 4 ft (1200 mm) 40W, and the 2 ft (600 mm) 20W. They are all of a standard size, 1¼ in. in diameter, and are used in both single and twin-tube fittings.

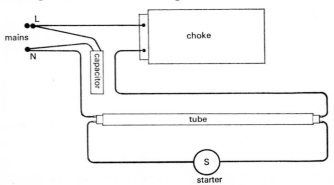

Fig. 8 Fluorescent tube circuits—a switch start single tube circuit

Fig. 9 Flourescent tube circuits (a) single tube quick-start circuit
(b) twin-tube switch start circuit

Both tubes in a twin-tube fitting switch on and off simultaneously but in the switch start type by removing the starter
switch of one, only one tube need be used, the second can remain
as a spare. The twin 20W tube fitting has a series circuit with the
tubes wired in series and both must work for either to operate
since they use a common choke. Should one tube fail both go out,
whereas the 40W and 60W twin tubes operate independently.

CIRCUIT ACCESSORIES

A starter switch, choke and a capacitor are the accessories and these vary with the type of circuit. The functions of choke and starter have already been explained. The capacitor is usually used for power factor correction and plays no significant part in the tube's operation. In some circuits, such as twin-tube series circuits, the capacitor performs a function and no power factor correction is necessary.

Power factor correction capacitors are made in various sizes to suit the circuit and any replacement must be identical to the original. They are required by the Electricity Board and any home constructed fluorescent fitting must include one, because the choke produces what is termed *wattless current* which is not recorded or measured on the electricity meter. This 'lagging' current is expressed as a percentage whereas tungsten filament lighting has what is termed unity power factor. A fluorescent choke reduces this to about 0·65 (lagging) and the Board requires it to be corrected or improved to at least 0·85 or 85% of unity which is the function of the capacitor. Some circuits produce a leading power factor, in excess of unity, which is dealt with by other means.

PELMET LIGHTING USING FLUORESCENT TUBES

Fluorescent tubes fixed behind the pelmet can be used quite effectively to illuminate the curtains when drawn. The tube or tubes, fixed to the pelmet board at a distance of 4–6 in. (200–300 mm) in front of the curtains will flood the whole of the curtain area with light. If set closer only the tops of the curtains are likely to be illuminated, but some experiment is usually necessary to get the optimum effect. The ends of the tube must extend a few inches beyond the width of the curtains, and if more than one tube is used to get the required length the joins must overlap to prevent 'breaks' or gaps in the overall light.

For downward lighting only, reflector tubes can be used and these must be fitted the correct way so that the internal reflector is on top when the tube is in position. Upward light, reflected from the ceiling, requires a pelmet with an open top.

The ballast gear, starter and pfc capacitor can be housed within the pelmet structure or positioned elsewhere by extending the circuit wiring. This and other types of supplementary lighting can be supplied from a spur of the ring circuit via a fused outlet, or from a lighting circuit. The switches can be local or remote as required.

CIRCULAR FLUORESCENT FITTINGS

These are fitted with circular tubes in diameters of: $8\frac{1}{4}$ in. (200 mm) 22W; 12 in. (300 mm) 32W; and 18 in. (400 mm) 40W. Some fittings have two tubes of different diameters. The circuits are usually switch start types and include choke, starter switch and pfc capacitor.

MINIATURE FLUORESCENT TUBES

'Mini-tubes', give high lumen output with low power consumption: roughly five times the light output of the equivalent in tungsten filament bulbs. In the home, their long life, low operating temperature and small size makes them suitable for many situations where a bulb or filament strip light would normally be used; for instance embodied in the control panel of a cooker.

They are made in four 'tones' of white—'White', 'Warmwhite', 'Daylight' and 'Natural'. Sizes are: 6 in. (150 mm) 4W; 9 in. (225 mm) 6W; 12 in. (300 mm); 8W and 21 in. (450 mm) 13W. Tube diameter is 16 mm and the lamp caps are mini bi-pin.

FAULT FINDING

Unlike a filament lamp, a fluorescent tube does not fail suddenly nor does it usually fail completely. It normally shows some form of life depending on the nature of the fault and whether it is in the tube or in a component. The behaviour of the tube under a fault is a good indication of the trouble.

The following table lists the more common faults, how they are diagnosed and rectified.

TABLE 4

Fluorescent Tube Failures

Tube behaviour	*Probable cause*
Tube appears completely dead.	Circuit fuse or fuse in fitting or plug blown; break in circuit wiring; or, if a switch-start circuit, a faulty lampholder contact or broken tube electrode.
Electrodes glow at each end but tube makes no attempt to start.	*Switch-start type:* If glow is white, faulty starter; if red, tube is at end of useful life. *Quick-start type:* Ineffective earth connection at metal fitting or to metal stripe of tube; or wrong type of tube. e.g. no metal stripe.
Tube glows at one end only when trying unsuccessfully to start.	*Switch-start type:* Lampholder connection at dead end of tube short-circuited. *Quick-start type:* Broken tube electrode or disconnection at dead end of tube.
Tube makes repeated but unsuccessful efforts to start.	Faulty starter; low mains voltage tube is very old. Twin-tube circuit: lampholder connections crossed.
Tube lights normally for a few seconds, then goes out and repeats.	Faulty starter; low mains voltage tube past its useful life, especially where it extinguishes with a shimmering effect.*
Tube lights up but at half brightness	Tube past its useful life.
Series twin-tube circuit i.e. two 20W 2 ft tubes: One tube extra bright, other tube not alight.	Starter faulty or is wrong type for the circuit.

*NB. A new tube sometimes lights with a shimmering effect. The tube is not faulty but soon settles down to normal working.

8 | Space Heating

Heat emitted by an electric space heater is either radiant heat or convected heat. Radiant heat is usually associated with visible 'red' elements but some panel heaters and storage radiators emit radiant heat from a 'black' surface. Convector heaters have elements usually operating at 'black' heat.

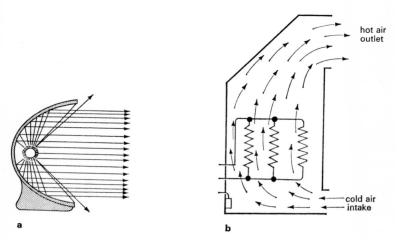

Fig. 10   Two forms of heat emission from electric fires
(a) radiant heat   (b) convected heat

The principal difference between the two is that radiant heat is the passage of heat from places of high temperature to places or objects of lower temperature without raising the temperature of the intervening air, convected heat is basically the production of warm air.

Although radiant electric heaters emit heat mainly by radiation and convectors mainly by convection, most radiant heaters emit some heat by convection and most convectors produce some radiant heat. The proportions depend on the particular design. Some electric heaters are designed as combined radiant/convector heaters and they contain both types of elements which operate at 'red' heat and 'black' heat respectively.

The traditional radiant heater or electric fire with exposed elements operating at red heat are designed mainly to supply a large measure of localised heat for short periods; a convector is used for a more overall continuous heat. However, the development of the low temperature panel heaters, skirting heaters and other 'low temperature' heaters which emit heat mainly by radiation, background heating is no longer confined to convectors.

Modern electric heaters are generally divided into two classes: direct-acting and storage.

Direct-acting heaters are so termed because they produce heat immediately they are switched on and cease to do so almost immediately after they are switched off. There are numerous types including focal point electric fires and background heaters most of which are available in portable and fixed versions. The focal point heater replaces the open coal fire and either stands in the grate or is built into a fireplace unit. Most models are radiant heaters fitted with fuel effect devices to imitate a coal or log solid fuel fire.

Storage heaters first store the heat when switched on and once charged with heat continue to expel it for some hours after they are switched off. A storage heater does not have to be filled with heat before it emits it but does so when the temperature of the outer casing is raised.

Background heaters, installed to pre-warm a room or to maintain it at a predetermined minimum temperature are usually of the skirting or panel type or oil-filled radiators. Free-standing convectors are also used for background heating. Fixed heaters are mainly various forms of panel heater, either radiant or convector, and are fixed to the wall at the appropriate height. Infrared radiant heaters, also fixtures, are especially suitable in bathrooms where they should be mounted high on the wall out of reach of a person using the bath or shower and in the kitchen and other rooms where space is limited and quick instant heating is required for fairly short periods.

Portable heaters cover almost every type of electric heater except storage. They are used for the main heating of a room or to provide local heating for short periods and obviously their principal advantage is that they can be carried from room to room as required.

RADIANT HEATERS
The most commonplace type of electric heater used in the home is the radiant electric fire. With loadings ranging from 500 watts to 3000 watts their elements operate at red heat and are usually exposed to touch but protected by a dress guard. Some are reflector fires: *rod elements*, termed pencil elements, are situated in front of a highly polished reflector which direct most of the heat forward into the room. Another form of radiant reflector fire is the infra-red heater which also has rod elements, but these are thinner and longer than the conventional type, are of lower loading and consist of a wire spiral element enclosed in a silica tube. The conventional rod element is a straight element wire wound on a fireclay former. They operate at a considerably higher temperature than the infra-red rod variety.

Other types of radiant electric fires have bar elements consisting of a brick-shaped fireclay former with a spiral wire element contained in a number of grooves, usually three or five.

Radiant fire elements have various loadings ranging from about 500 watts up to 1000 watts. Heaters in excess of 1000 watts have two or more elements. Loadings of infra-red rod elements are usually under 1000 watts each and the lengths range from 20 in. to 24 in. (500–600 mm). Loadings of the conventional rod elements are usually 1000 watts and the lengths are about 11 in. (275 mm). Shorter rod elements of lower loadings are fitted to some models. Fire bar elements are mainly of 1000 watts each.

Another radiant reflector heater is the bowl fire which has a parabolic polished reflector and a tubular or globe shaped ele-

D

ment consisting of a fireclay former with a spiral groove containing the spiral wire element.

Multi-element radiant heaters have built-in switches to provide variation in heat output: one element is usually connected direct to the flexible cord of a portable fire. A 1-bar fire has no integral switch; a 2-bar fire has an integral switch for the second element; a 3-bar fire has two integral switches, one for the second element and one for the third. The exception is a fuel effect fire. The fuel effect indicates when the heater is switched on, and all elements are operated by individual built-in switches. Fixed radiant fires (panel fires) have switches for all elements.

CONVECTOR HEATERS

The convector is box shaped and contains an element unit operating at 'black' heat. With its comparatively low surface temperature this unit heats the air around it, which then rises and flows out through a grille into the room. This air is replaced by colder air which is drawn in through the base of the cabinet thus creating a continuous flow. The flow continues until the incoming air reaches the cutting out temperature of the integral thermostat. Some convectors have no thermostat and have to be controlled manually; alternatively a room thermostat can be wired into the circuit. Loadings vary from 500 watts to 3000 watts and the cabinet contains a pilot light which produces a warm glow.

FAN HEATERS

The fan heater is a convector which drives air over elements instead of relying on natural convection. This method enables a greater heat output from a smaller casing because the fan keeps the elements at a fairly low temperature. The fan has a separate switch and can be operated without the heaters and is used as such in hot weather. The heater, however, cannot be switched on without the fan because the elements would become too hot and damage the unit. The heat output can be varied by means of switches, giving a maximum loading of 3000 watts (some models have lower wattage elements). The unit contains a pilot light, usually a neon indicator.

COMBINED RADIATOR-CONVECTORS

Commonly called 'radiant convectors' these contain radiant elements operating at red heat and a cabinet convector containing a heater unit operating at 'black' heat. The units can be operated together or independently each being separately switched.

FUEL EFFECT FIRES

The traditional fuel effect fire is a radiant heat (convectors as well now) with the addition of an imitation coal or log unit formerly of treated wire gauze but now of plastic. The fuel effect is illuminated by one or more coloured lamps (bulbs), over which are mounted spinners which simulate flames and smoke when driven by warm convected currents of air produced by the lamp.

Some modern versions are motor driven and produce a variety of dramatic effects. The fuel effect can be operated independently of the heating elements so it can be used on a warm evening or on a dull warm day. It also functions as a pilot light and indicates when the circuit switch is on and the flexible cord is 'live'.

TUBULAR HEATERS

Available in lengths from 2 ft to 17 ft (0·600–5·100 m) tubular heaters are made of steel or light alloy, are 2 in. in diameter and contain a spiral element supported on mica discs fitted to a spine running throughout the length of the tube. The standard loading is 60 watts per foot run and the tubes operate at a surface temperature of about 180°F. Higher loadings are available and these operate at a higher surface temperature.

The tubes are usually fixed at or near skirting level by means of brackets or they can stand on the floor or be fixed to it. They produce a wide distribution of heat and are especially suitable for background heating. They can be operated as single tubes or can be built-up into banks of two or more tiers by adding brackets and fitting a connecting bar. The heat from a single tube is mainly radiant, but as more tubes are added to form a bank the air flow is increased and more heat is produced by convection with a corresponding reduction in radiant heat. A tubular heater installation can be controlled automatically by a room thermostat and where desired can also be time controlled. Special heaters of this type are also made for use in the greenhouse. The electricity supply to a tube or bank of tubes can be from a fused connection unit or from a 13A fused plug and socket-outlet on the ring circuit.

A disadvantage of tubular heaters is their low loading. For example to obtain a load of 2000 watts about 34 ft of tube is required at the standard loading of 60 watts per ft. Using tubes in banks, however, largely offsets this. Their chief merits are flexibility and wide heat distribution and a comparatively low outlay.

OIL-FILLED RADIATORS
Similar in shape and style to the conventional hot water radiator, the oil-filled electric radiator has a thermostatically controlled immersion element and is excellent as a background heater placed under a window or in any other convenient position.

It is extremely safe in operation, has no exposed elements and can therefore be fixed in a bathroom. Versions are available with a towel rail fitted which on some models is detachable.

WALL PANEL HEATERS
Wall panel heaters are made in various sizes, styles and loadings. They operate at a low surface temperature and can be touched without risk of scorching. Suitable for most rooms and in particular the hall, landing and bathroom, they are an alternative to oil-filled electric radiators. The elements are totally enclosed, usually embedded in the panel and are therefore extremely safe. They can be connected to a fused socket outlet by flexible cord except in the bathroom where socket-outlets are banned.

9 | Electric Storage Heating (Electric Central Heating)

An electric storage heater is basically a block or blocks of thermal storage refractory material containing electric elements, and enclosed in a metal casing with thermal insulation between the refractory and the casing.

They are designed to operate in conjunction with the 'White Meter' electricity tariff or on other off-peak tariffs and are switched into circuit during an overnight period of about eight hours. The switch-on period starts about 11 p.m. and ends at about 7 a.m. during which time the refractory block is 'charged' with heat. Actual switching times vary in different areas but in all cases it is an overnight period when cheaper electricity becomes available.

The stored heat is emitted during the 16-hour day period though heat is also emitted during the charging period. When fully charged at switch-off time heat output is at its maximum, but tends to taper off throughout the day.

There are two principal types: the electric storage radiator, most commonly used; and the storage fan heater which contains a fan to expel warm air out through a grille.

Electric storage radiators are made in a range of sizes (electrical loadings) starting at 1·5 kW up to a maximum 3·375kW. Storage fan heaters start at 3kW and cover a range of loadings up to about 8kW.

STORAGE RADIATORS

The heat from a storage radiator is emitted from the metal casing which is maintained at a fairly even temperature for much of the day. This is controlled by the casing's thermal insulation which ensures that heat is not radiated too rapidly.

Unlike that of a direct-acting electric heater, the kW loading does not represent the rate of heat output though it bears some relation to it. Loadings vary with the size (bulk or storage capacity) of the heater: the higher the electrical loading the greater the heat storage capacity. Since a storage heater has only about eight hours to accept heat the rate of charge has to be greater for the higher capacity storage blocks. This means a higher electrical loading.

As a storage heater of higher electrical loading usually contains more heat (when fully charged) but has the same daytime period as all others to expel it, naturally it follows that the rate of heat output must be higher. You therefore choose your storage heaters according to the kW loading, provided they are of the same type when comparing loadings, and you accept that the loading is not the rate of heat output. For example a 3·375kW storage radiator can usually be expected to emit heat at a continuous rate of 1000 watts for much of the day. The length of this period varies, is stated by the makers and is usually for the first 10–12 hours of the day starting at the switch-off time of 7 a.m.

Storage electric radiators are essentially continuous heaters compared with direct-acting heaters which are switched on and off as required. As such they keep the walls at a higher temperature than that outside and generally provide overall comfort in common with other central heating systems.

The heat output cannot be adjusted by the householder but there is an input controller to vary the amount of heat stored overnight which, to some extent, influences the output rate next day. For much of the winter the input controller is at a maximum but in mild weather a lower setting can be satisfactory. To reduce costs, individual heaters can be switched off in rooms not in immediate use but it is necessary to remember that a heater switched off overnight will not supply heat the following day. Some models have an adjustable damper to provide a boost of heat in the early evening when the rate of heat output has tapered off from its daytime maximum. Either manually or automatically controlled this damper usually contains a device which prevents the householder from opening it too early in the day and losing most of the stored heat.

STORAGE FAN HEATERS
These have more thermal insulation than the storage radiator and as a result their casing temperature is much lower and the output of radiated heat significantly smaller. Heat output is mainly con-vected warm air. The householder is therefore able to choose the times when the heater is to expel its stored heat either manually by operating the fan switch on the heater, or automatically by means of room thermostats or time-switches (or both) wired into the fan circuits. Devices are usually incorporated to prevent the householder expelling most of the stored heat early in the day.

POSITIONING
Storage heaters generally should be situated where they will cope with the coldest spots in the rooms. Preferably they should be set near a window, but at right angles to it so that the heat is directed across the cold area, but not under the window where much of the heat is likely to be lost via the glass.

CIRCUIT WIRING
Since all storage heaters are switched on at the same time it is necessary that each is supplied from an individual circuit origi-nating at a separate fuseway in the consumer unit. The circuit should be of 20A current rating so that the largest size radiator likely to be installed can be connected to it. Cable used is 2·5 sq mm twin-core and earth pvc sheathed house wiring cable. Each circuit terminated at a 20A double-pole switch with a cord outlet fixed near the storage radiator which is connected to this switch by 3-core heat resisting 3-core sheathed flex. The switch can to advantage have a neon indicator but it is not essential. Four storage heaters with their four circuits would be supplied from a 4-way consumer unit, but if the immersion heater is also to be supplied from the time-switch controlled consumer unit, an additional fuseway will be required.

Fig. 11   Circuit wiring for storage radiators

Where there are to be fewer than four storage heaters or fewer than three plus immersion heater a 4-way consumer unit should still be fitted as the 60A switch with this unit is necessary to supply the load. Where no more than two storage radiators are installed and each has a loading not in excess of 3kW they can alternatively be supplied from a 30A circuit wired in 4 sq mm cable. Since the fuse rating will be 30A the outlet to each heater must be fused. (These have a current rating of only 13A which restricts each storage heater to 3 kW.) The consumer unit can be fitted with miniature circuit breakers instead of fuses, and are preferable.

As already mentioned storage heaters operate during off-peak

Consumer unit with fuses (*Wylex*)

Consumer unit with miniature circuit breakers (*Crabtree*)

Left : rewirable fuse (*MEM*)   *Right :* cartridge fuse (*MEM*)

Left : miniature circuit breaker (*Lupus*)   *Right :* earth leakage circuit breaker (*Allen West*)

13A fused plug (*Crabtree*)

Left : modern ceiling rose showing terminals and connections (*Rock*)
Right : encased ceiling rose

Left : shaver supply unit (*H.H. Electrical*)   *Right :* fitting immersion heater into flange of hot water cylinder

Dual immersion heater (*Backer*)

Side entry immersion heater

hours, the time-switch necessary is provided by the Electricity Board who connect the leads from the consumer unit to it. That is why a separate consumer unit is needed to supply only those circuits which are to be current restricted for the 8-hour night period. All others, including lighting and the ring circuit, are connected to the general purpose consumer unit to receive current continuously. Storage heaters are not connected to or supplied from a ring circuit because such a circuit is designed for portable and certain fixed appliances which because they are used intermittently carry very little risk of overloading the circuit. A single storage heater having a loading not in excess of 3kW can be connected to a ring circuit provided the householder is prepared to switch it on and off at the beginning and end of the cheap-rate period.

A storage fan heater has to be supplied from two circuits: one supplies the heater and is connected to the restricted-hour consumer unit as for a storage radiator; the other supplies the fan from the unrestricted 24-hour supply so that it can be operated at any time during the day when the heater is not receiving current. This requires a special outlet switch which must be an isolating switch to negate the heater circuit and the fan circuit simultaneously. The one to use is the MK 25A linked switch which has two flex outlets and made with and without neon indicators.

As the fan takes only a few watts of electricity it may be supplied from either the lighting circuit or from the ring circuit via a fused connection unit. A number of fans may be run off the one circuit. Where a room thermostat or a time-switch is used this is wired into the fan circuit. Each fan can be controlled independently, or one room thermostat and/or time-switch can control a number of heater fans.

ELECTRICAIRE HEATING
Electricaire is basically a large storage fan heater centrally situated in the house which provides warm air to all or most rooms, via a system of ducting and grilles like other warm-air central heating systems. The unit is available in a number of sizes having loadings

of 10–16 kW. For the average home a 10·8 kW model is a suitable and fairly common loading. The circuit for this size unit has a 45A current rating and the cable terminates in a control unit which contains a heater switch and a switch for the fan which has neon indicators. The unit can be sited in any convenient position.

Although not termed Electricaire units, some of the larger storage fan heaters have facilities for supplying two or more adjacent rooms by means of stub ducting and shutters. The difference between these and Electricaire room heaters is that they supply each room alternatively but not usually simultaneously. Selective supply of warm air to individual rooms can also be effected with the Electricaire system by means of adjustable grilles.

CENTRALEC HEATING

This is the term given to the new wet system of electric central heating. The heater is a modified Electricaire unit containing an air-to-water heat exchanger to supply hot water to a conventional system of pipes and radiators. As the heat is stored overnight during the cheap rate electricity period, costs compare favourably with the conventional boiler using other fuels.

FLOOR WARMING

This is a sophisticated heating system which uses electric warming cables in the concrete screed of a solid floor normally installed during the building construction. It is especially attractive in blocks of flats, where space is usually at a premium, for this form of heating occupies no space at all. It is a night-storage system but normally requires a midday boost which for new installations is supplied at the higher (day) rate. Costs though are comparable with other forms of electric storage heating. Almost any type of floor covering can be laid on the warmed floor including wall-to-wall carpet. Maximum floor temperature which occurs at night, is about 80°F. (26°C).

CEILING HEATING

This is a recent development for domestic use and there are two principal types. With one type the warming wires are installed before the ceiling is fixed or plastered. The other comprises panels containing the warming wires which form the finished ceiling or can be fixed to an existing ceiling.

The system is really a ceiling version of floor warming but although being classed as electric central heating it is non-storage. The heat emission is by radiation which, near floor level, creates convected currents of warm air that circulate throughout the room.

10 | Electric Water Heating

There are three principal types of electric water heater suitable for installation in the home: instantaneous; storage; and immersion. Instantaneous water heaters supply showers and sinks. Storage water heaters are used for all purposes, especially where large quantities of hot water are required. Immersion heaters are used in conjunction with a solid-fuel system and are fitted into the conventional hot water storage tank. They are also used as the sole means of providing hot water where there is no solid fuel boiler.

INSTANTANEOUS WATER HEATERS

These have no storage vessel but heat the water as it flows through the unit. Usually it can be connected direct to the cold water mains, the outflow of hot water being controlled by an inlet valve. When the valve is opened the cold mains water under pressure flows into the heater unit where it is heated and flows out through an open spout or from a shower unit. The electric current to the heater element is controlled by an automatic diaphragm switch which is operated by the water pressure: when the water flows the switch is turned on, and off when the water flow is stopped.

Water temperature varies with the rate of flow: the greater the flow the lower the temperature and vice versa. It also depends on the electrical loading of the heater elements: the output of hot water from a 6kW instantaneous water heater will be almost double that from a 3kW unit.

When choosing an instantaneous water heater the loading is therefore very important. Various loadings are: 3kW, 4kW, 5kW, 6kW and 7kW. A 3kW is used for hand washing and is fitted over a hand basin; the 4kW and 5kW models are used for supplying the kitchen sink; and the 5kW and 6kW models are used for showers. The 7kW model is intended especially for supplying two outlets in conjunction with a special 2-way faucet valve.

Makes vary in design and styles of course. Some models consist of a basic unit, in alternative loadings, and can be fitted with hand-washing sprays, showering units and other accessories. Some such as the Santon 'Imp' is designed simply for hand washing. Another model, made by Sadia is a press-button unit.

All have an open outlet and must not be plumbed to a closed tap. The pressure of the cold water supply is important, mains pressure is usually adequate but if supplied from a cold water storage tank at least a 7 ft head of water is necessary.

The electrical circuit too is important. A 3kW model may be run off a 13A fused outlet fed from a ring circuit, but if the outlet is in the bathroom there must not be a plug and socket, but a fused connection unit which, if containing a switch, must be out of reach of a person using the bath or shower. A 4kW unit requires a 20A circuit and 4kW, 5kW, 6kW and 7kW models require a 30A circuit, and a 30A outlet switch.

STORAGE WATER HEATERS

Basically these are a hot water storage vessel containing the water immersion heater to heat it, a thermostat to control the temperature, thermal insulation to prevent undue heat losses, and inlet valve to control the flow and a hot water outlet pipe.

There are three principal types: (i) the *free outlet displacement* type for direct connection to the mains water system; (ii) the *pressure* type which is supplied from a cold water storage cistern; (iii) the *cistern* type which is a self-contained unit, complete with its own cold water storage cistern that can usually be connected to the cold water mains supply.

FREE OUTLET STORAGE WATER HEATERS

These are single-point water heaters for use at the sink or wash-basin, with larger models for the conventional bath. They are similar to the instantaneous water heater except that the water is pre-heated and stored for future use.

Capacities range from 1 gallon to 20 gallons, but unlike the instantaneous type, the heater elements have a maximum loading of 3kw and can be as low as 1kW. The quantity of hot water which can be drawn off at any one time is limited by the storage capacity of the hot water vessel. When this amount has been drawn off it is necessary to wait until more water is heated, and time taken to do this is termed the 'recovery period'. The rate of recovery depends on the electrical loading of the element. When buying a storage water heater choose one which has sufficient capacity for one draw-off with a recovery rate quick enough to meet subsequent demands.

The thermostat setting, which determines the storage temperature of the water, also has a bearing on the amount of hot water available and is usually adjustable from about 90°F (33°C) to 180°F (84°C). For washing dishes you require a water temperature of 140°F (60°C). If the thermostat is set at 140°F (60°C) a 1½-gallon sink water heater will provide 1½ gallons of water at 140°F (60°C) at one draw-off and no more. If, however, the thermostat is set at 160°F (72°C) the 1½ gallons from the water heater mixed with cold water from the tap will provide about 2 gallons of water at 140°F (60°C). Similarly, for hand washing where you need water at 110°F (44°C) you can get nearly 3 gallons from a 1½-gallon water heater when mixed with cold water.

Although a high storage temperature provides more hot water at usable temperature at one draw-off, there are disadvantages. Heat losses are greater for these are proportional to the storage temperature. Scaling is also more likely: in very hard water areas the storage temperature should not be higher than 140°F (60°C) but in very soft water areas a storage temperature of up to 180°F (84°C) is permissible, but the heat losses may be excessive. Generally, therefore, the storage temperature—the setting of the thermostat—should not exceed 160°F (72°C) and the size (capacity) of the water heater chosen accordingly.

Storage water heaters suitable for the kitchen sink are available in about six sizes from $1\frac{1}{3}$ gallons to 3 gallons capacity. They have electrical loadings of 3kW and alternative loadings of 1kW and 3kW. Where a 13A outlet on the ring circuit is available, or a separate 15A circuit can be wired, the 3kW loading should be chosen to obtain the quickest recovery. For normal sink requirements a $1\frac{1}{3}$-gallon or $1\frac{1}{2}$-gallon model fitted with a 3kW element is adequate. The recovery from cold of a $1\frac{1}{3}$-gallon 3kW water heater is eight minutes and that of a $1\frac{1}{2}$-gallon model ten minutes. The recovery of a $1\frac{1}{3}$-gallon fitted with a 1kW element is twenty-four minutes and that of a $1\frac{1}{2}$-gallon thirty minutes.

Where larger quantities of hot water are required at the sink a $2-2\frac{1}{2}$-gallon size should be chosen. For the wash-basin a $1\frac{1}{3}$-gallon or $1\frac{1}{2}$-gallon model is adequate but these should have a 3kW loading to ensure good quantities of hot water at peak times. To supply a bath you need a 15-gallon or 20-gallon size. The latter will supply sufficient hot water for two baths in fairly rapid succession, for 12 gallons of hot water at about 160°F (72°C) require about the same quantity of cold to 'fill' the bath with water at 110°F (44°C).

Installing a sink water heater
A displacement—or free—outlet water heater needs very little plumbing. The water heater is fixed to the wall over the sink in a position where its swivel outlet spout will direct the hot water into the sink or washing up bowl. The cold water inlet of the unit is connected to the mains supply by a short length of $\frac{1}{2}$ in. (13 mm) copper or plastic pipe. The simplest method of doing this is to unscrew the cold water tap, screw in a TEE fitting and refit the tap to the TEE. From the TEE runs a short length of pipe to the inlet of the water heater. For the electrical wiring a length of 1·5 sq. mm 3-core sheathed flex is connected to the 13A fused outlet, which is a switched fused connection unit or a fused plug and socket-outlet. The switch is usually left 'ON' and preferably the fused unit has a neon indicator.

Hot water is drawn off by opening the inlet valve. There is a short delay between opening the valve and the hot water flowing, and a corresponding delay when closing the valve and the flow of hot water ceasing. This is because the free outlet water heater has a non-drip device, which prevents water dripping from the spout as it expands when it is heated.

Under no circumstances must the outlet be plumbed to a closed tap. If it were the water, as it is heated, would build up a pressure and should the thermostat 'stick' in the closed position the water heater could explode.

A WATER-BOIL SINK HEATER

Normally a sink electric water heater will not provide boiling water (water at 140°F–180°F (60°C to 84°C) can be used for culinary purposes and brought to the boil in a kettle or cooking vessel) though one make can do so when required. This is the Creda 'Corvette', sometimes termed a wall kettle, which has a non-lagged glass water storage vessel with a capacity just under one gallon. The vessel is graduated in pints on a scale and is filled from the cold water tap by a rubber hose. No plumbing is therefore required and only the quantity of water needed is run into the vessel which can be anything from two cups up to its full capacity.

The temperature can be adjusted and switched to boiling when required. When the water reaches boiling point an audible warning is given.

This, like most sink water heaters, can be connected by its 3-core flex to a switched fused connection unit, or to a fused plug and socket-outlet. But like any electric water heater when fitted in a bathroom it must, under no circumstances, be supplied from a plug and socket-outlet. A switched fused outlet may normally be fixed in the bathroom for this purpose but if the switch should be within reach of someone using the bath or a shower it must either be cord operated from the ceiling or a wall switch positioned outside the bathroom door.

PRESSURE TYPE WATER HEATERS

This type of electric storage water heater is similar to the free outlet displacement type but must be supplied from a cold water system and requires a vent pipe. It will supply one or a number of hot water taps.

The water in the hot water storage vessel is constantly under pressure—the pressure being that of the secondary cold water supply which is determined by the height of the ball valve in the cold water storage cistern in relation to the water heater and the taps it supplies. Plumbing for the water heater and draw-off system is similar to that of the conventional domestic hot water system and storage tank heated from a solid-fuel boiler, but in this case there is no boiler or flow and return pipes.

A cold water feed pipe has to be run from the cold water storage cistern, usually in the loft, down to the cold water inlet of the water heater. A hot water draw-off pipe is run from the hot water outlet, usually on top of the water heater, to feed the various hot water taps. From this draw-off system a vent pipe is run to above the cold water feed tank and is directed down into the tank. As the water in the hot water vessel is under pressure hot water is drawn off in the conventional manner simply by opening or turning on the hot water taps.

These water heaters are made in a wide range of sizes from about five gallons up to about 100 gallons for domestic use and larger for commercial use. The size chosen depends on requirements. For a one-outlet installation a 5-gallon model would be adequate but it is better to choose one which will supply all or most of the hot water draw-off positions. For the average home a 20-gallon size is usually adequate and will supply the three taps at the sink, bath and wash-basin. A 30-gallon model is also available; most are dual units but some have one element which heats the full contents of the storage vessel.

Especially suitable and designed for the home is the dual type. This has a storage capacity of 20 gallons and it can usually stand on the floor adjacent to the sink and under the draining board. This heater has two element units: one is fitted near the top in the side of the unit and heats about six gallons of water; the other, also a side-entry type, is fitted near the base of the vessel to heat the

E

full contents. With some models both elements have a 3kW loading and are controlled by a change-over switch so that both elements cannot operate simultaneously. The switch is marked 'SINK' and 'BATH'—the lower element being switched on when the full contents are heated for a bath or other purposes and the top element being switched on for normal hot water requirements at the sink and wash-basin.

Some models have a 2kW lower element and a 1kW upper element so that when switched to 'BATH' both elements are in circuit with a total loading of 3kW. In either case the maximum loading is 3kW enabling the water heater to be supplied from a 15A circuit. This must be a separate circuit; not a spur from a ring circuit because it is a continuously operated water heater and would deprive the ring circuit of 3kW, which would then not be available for portable appliances.

When these dual water heaters are operated on the 'White Meter' tariff a modification of the wiring is made so that the full contents are heated overnight at the cheaper rate, but during the day the housewife can switch on the top element should she need additional hot water. An extra external circuit is required for this daytime facility.

CISTERN TYPE WATER HEATERS

This is a self-contained electric water heater unit for supplying hot water to a number of taps when there is no secondary supply of hot water available from a cold water feed tank. It is made in various capacities from 12 gallons to 30 gallons: the 20-gallon unit being necessary if a bath as well as a sink and wash-basin are supplied. It can usually be fitted on the wall above the bath remembering to situate it above the highest draw-off tap because the supply of hot water is motivated by gravity. The wall must be strong enough to support the weight of the stored water as well as the weight of the water heater unit. Some models are floor mounted.

The unit consists of a thermal-insulated hot water storage vessel containing an immersion heater, a cold water feed cistern, with a

Fig. 12 Water heater arrangements (a) alternating immersion heater
arrangements (b) 20 gallon under-sink electric water heater
(c) cistern-type electric water heater

ball valve and a self-contained venting system. The whole unit
is inside a sheet steel case. Plumbing involves running a cold water
feed pipe (normally direct from the mains) to the feed tank; taking
an overflow pipe to the outside of the building; and running the
hot water draw-off piping to all the taps. It should be fitted near
an outside wall for the overflow pipe; this may be on either side
of the unit—the mains feed pipe being connected to the other
side.

When choosing the position, sufficient headroom must be
allowed for access to the ball valve (the immersion heater is bottom
entry whereas the floor mounted type has side entry immersion

heaters.) Where there is no other suitable position for a cistern-type water heater it may be fixed in the roof space or attic, this is sometimes necessary in a bungalow to provide an adequate head of water.

Electrical loadings of these heaters are not more than 3kW enabling one to be supplied from a 15A outlet.

IMMERSION HEATERS

An electric immersion heater is a convenient way of providing hot water from the conventional storage cylinder or tank, operated either in conjunction with a solid-fuel boiler or as the sole means of water heating. They are made in a wide range of types, lengths and electrical loadings.

In its most simple form, an immersion heater consists of a mineral-insulated metal sheathed element similar to that of an electric kettle but different in shape. Element lengths range from about 11 in. to 36 in. A thermostat is usually fitted in the heater head but it is optional and most are of the rod or stem type, adjustable over a range of temperatures from about 90°F to 180°F (33–84°C), the non-stem type have fixed temperatures set during manufacture. The adjustable thermostat should be set at about 140°F (60°C) in hard water districts and may be up to about 180°F (84°C) where water is soft and scaling unlikely. To reduce heat losses to a reasonable level even when the tank is well lagged the storage temperature and therefore the setting of the thermostat should not be higher than 160°F (72°C).

Immersion heaters are screwed into a flange fitted in the wall of the tank. This flange, and the immersion heater head, has a $2\frac{1}{4}$ in. BSPT thread (British Standard Pipe Thread) being the diameter of the bore of the pipe and not of the flange which should be borne in mind when the hole in the tank wall is cut.

Either the top of the tank or the side wall are good positions for it. Top entry is normal for the copper cylinder and side entry for the rectangular tank and where there is not enough headroom for inserting or withdrawing a top entry immersion heater.

With top entry it is important that the element extends to within a few inches of the base of the cylinder so that the whole of the hot water is heated. Allowance must be made if the base is concave. A side entry immersion heater must be fitted as near to the base as possible for this reason also as water below it will not heat.

To heat and to maintain the temperature of the whole tankful of water can be wasteful when only small quantities are run off during the day because heat losses are roughly proportional to the quantity of water stored at a given temperature. Known as *standing losses* these are highest when no water is being drawn off, for then the temperature remains at the maximum set by the thermostat. To reduce this a twin element or dual top entry immersion heater can be fitted which has two elements, one long enough to reach to the bottom of the cylinder and one shorter to heat just a small quantity of water at the top. The short element is usually about 12 in. (300 mm) but there are other lengths, the longer element is 32–36 in. (800–900 mm) depending on the size or capacity of the cylinder.

Loadings range from 1kW to 3kW, and the latter is for a single-element immersion heater. Each element of a twin- or dual-element immersion heater can be 3kW provided they are controlled by a change-over switch to prevent them both from being switched into circuit together.

Twin or dual-element?
The difference between these two immersion heaters is that the twin-element has one thermostat to control both elements, whereas the dual-element version has two separately controlled elements on the one heater head.

For most applications a twin-element unit is suitable but where each has to be supplied from a separate circuit the dual version is necessary. An example is where the supply is on the 'White Meter' tariff, when the longer element must be on a time-controlled off-peak circuit and the short element on the unrestricted circuit.

Installing an immersion heater
Equipment required for fitting a top entry immersion heater

into a conventional copper hot water storage cylinder not already fitted with a $2\frac{1}{4}$ in. BSPT boss or flange is: one Essex-type single hole $2\frac{1}{4}$ in. BSPT (57·2 mm) flange, the immersion heater, a tank cutter or hole saw and a $2\frac{1}{4}$ in. (57·2 mm) BSPT ring spanner. If the cylinder is of the direct type, containing no heat exchanger the job is quite straightforward.

First cut off the mains water supply and drain the tank; this requires a tap in the system below the level of the tank's base. Using the tank cutter make the necessary hole in the top of the tank on the dome, about midway between the draw-off pipe and the rim of the dome.

Insert a cane or rod into the cylinder to check there is no obstruction. Screw in the flange according to the makers' instructions, ensuring that you do not let the inner section fall into the bottom of the tank, and that you fit the flange washers to prevent a leak. Check the length of the long element by means of the rod. Tighten the flange using a ring spanner or a wrench. Screw in the immersion heater and tighten in the same way.

Close the drain tap and turn on the water to remove air locks if present. Run off some water to check that the system is operating and that the tank is full. Check for weeping (slight leakage) at the flange, and if there is any it will be necessary to unscrew the immersion heater and introduce some Boss's White or similar jointing compound into the joint. Tighten the immersion heater again and the weeping should have ceased.

If the cylinder is of the indirect type it will be necessary to ensure that the immersion heater will not be fouled by the heat exchanger or calorifier. (An indirect type is recognised by the outlet and inlets which it has in addition to flow and return pipe connections.) The immersion heater must pass perpendicularly into the cylinder and special flanges are available for this. First drill the hole for the flange and check it with a rod. If an immersion heater cannot then be inserted fix the Essex flange and fit a plug to seal the hole. Some tanks are sold already fitted with the plugged flange.

To fit an immersion heater into a rectangular tank is relatively easy, for these tanks have removable hand hole covers. Before removing the cover buy a replacement gasket. To remove the cover release all the stud screws and clean the old jointing compound from the surface of the tank. Check inside for rusting and remove any sludge. Having decided on the best position for the immersion heaters (ensure no pipes will protrude) fit the flange or flanges, then the heaters and replace the cover.

When an immersion heater is fitted into an indirect tank or cylinder it is necessary to have a valve in the central heating, or secondary system, to prevent the hot water from circulating through it and so causing unnecessary heat losses and wasting electricity. When the installation is finally complete fit a lagging jacket on to the tank so that heat losses are reduced to a minimum.

IMMERSION HEATER CIRCUIT WIRING AND CONTROLS

An immersion heater, irrespective of its type, must be controlled by an isolating double-pole switch fitted within reach of a person attending to the heater or thermostat. This is usually a double-pole 20A switch marked 'WATER HEATER' and it can have a neon indicator. The wiring is a 15A circuit from a 15/20A fuseway in the consumer unit. Special controls are required for a dual-immersion heater and when supplied from two circuits a linked switch is needed. Another variant is a remote control in the kitchen to switch the heater to 'BATH'. The Hotpoint Twimerser has this facility. Alternatively, the change-over switch can be on the heater head itself and hand switched as necessary. Remote control is also possible with two separate main switches: one containing an isolating device at the water heater, this being the master switch, and the other in the kitchen. Both have neon indicators which go on and off together as the switches are operated.

For the 'White Meter' tariff there are special controls some of which enable the housewife to over-ride the time control. One, the 'Backer', is a kit containing two immersion heaters. If a bath is wanted during the day there is a 'One-shot' control which enables the whole tankful of water to be heated, after which it switches off and reverts the system to automatic timed control.

OFF-PEAK STORAGE ELECTRIC WATER HEATERS

These are special jumbo size water storage heaters designed for the householder to take full advantage of off-peak cheaper electricity. They can be adapted to the 'White Meter' requirements and provide an adequate supply of hot water to the household.

HOME IMPROVEMENT GRANTS

When you have no bathroom and no room which can be converted into one you can install a shower cabinet fitted with an instantaneous water heater or a shower storage water heater, which can be in the hall, landing, kitchen, bedroom or elsewhere. As this will be the only 'bathroom' in the house it will probably qualify for a government home improvement grant. You should make enquiries about a grant before buying the cabinet and water heater.

11 | Wiring Systems

Most domestic circuits are wired in flat twin-core and earth pvc cable of various conductor sizes according to the current rating of the circuit. Some sections are wired in flat 3-core and earth sheathed cable, these being principally 2-way and intermediate switching circuits where one or more lights are controlled from three or more switch positions. A flat twin and earth sheathed cable comprises two insulated conductors, and one non-insulated conductor. One of the insulated conductors has black pvc insulation; the other has red, with the non-insulated conductor situated between them throughout the length of the cable.

The red conductor is used for the live wire and the black is used as the neutral. In a lighting circuit the black conductor is also used as the live conductor where it is the return wire from the switch, this being termed the *switch wire* of the circuit. To distinguish it from the black neutral wire the ends of a black insulated conductor when used as a switch wire have to be enclosed in a length of red sleeving. This is, however, not always done, so it is necessary to check the wires when replacing switches and lighting fittings.

The non-insulated conductor of a sheathed cable is the earth continuity conductor of the circuit. Where this is bared of its sheathing at switches, light fittings, socket outlets and joint boxes the ends are enclosed in green pvc sleeving which provides the necessary insulation.

Three-core and earth flat pvc sheathed cable used in house wiring consists of three pvc insulated conductors and one which is non-insulated. One conductor is coloured red, another is yellow and the third is blue. The non-insulated conductor is situated between the yellow and blue conductors throughout the length of the cable. The colours represent the different phases of a three-phase electricity supply system but have no significance when used in ordinary house wiring circuits. However, when the cable is used to link 2-way switches of 2-way switching circuits, and the three or more switches of an intermediate switching circuit, the colours can be used to distinguish the various wires and connections at the switches. (The bared end of the earth conductor is enclosed in green pvc sleeving at each switch.)

Although house wiring cables usually have copper conductors, two other materials are sometimes used: aluminium and copper coated aluminium. Aluminium is not used very much now because it sometimes corrodes at joint and terminal connections and as such does not comply with regulations. Copper coated aluminium is, however, used widely as an alternative to all-copper and is sold under various trade names. Its advantage is lower cost.

CABLE SIZES

Until 1971 conductors of house wiring cables were made in imperial sizes but have now been replaced by metric sizes. Most of the cables in existing houses are of the old imperial size but all additional wiring must now be with the equivalent metric size cables. Some cable conductors have changed since the introduction of the metric system: the three most commonly used for house wiring now have single-strand conductors whereas only one, which was the smallest size imperial cable, was like this. The next two imperial sizes had 3-strand conductors and the remainder had 7 strands each. When extending existing circuits therefore it is often necessary to join new single-strand conductors to the 3-strand and 7-strand type. This does not usually create any problem but it is something you should know. The various sizes of cables, both imperial and metric, with their equivalent current ratings are given in Table 5. Very large cables sometimes used to connect an installation to the Electricity Board's meter have 19-strand conductors, but only in rare cases will it apply to a metric cable installation.

CABLES USED FOR CIRCUITS

Sizes used in the home installation are: 1 sq. mm (formerly 1/·044) for lighting circuits; 1·5 sq. mm (formerly 3/·029) an alternative for lighting circuits and also used for 15A circuits supplying a single 13A socket-outlet or connection unit; 2·5 sq. mm (formerly 7/·029) for ring circuits, for 20A radial power circuits and for 20A circuits which supply storage heaters and other apparatus; 4 sq. mm (formerly 7/·036) for 30A radial power circuits, for instantaneous electric water heaters and other single-outlet circuits of this current rating. For a cooker circuit either 6 sq. mm or 10 sq. mm is used which replace 7/·044 and 7/·052 imperial size cables.

LIGHTING CIRCUITS
A lighting circuit using flat twin and earth pvc sheathed cable can be wired in two ways or a mixture of both. One method is the

Fig. 13　Connections for a loop-in ceiling rose

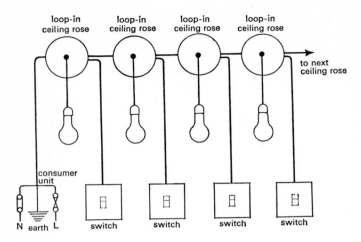

Fig. 14   Wiring a lighting circuit: loop-in system

loop-in system which is the more popular. The other is the joint box system which is used for surface wiring and where loop-in wiring is not practicable—for example, for wiring to wall lights which have no ceiling roses or loop-in facilities.

The loop-in system

With this system (Fig. 14) a flat twin and earth pvc sheathed cable runs from a 5A fuse in the consumer unit or fuse board to the live and neutral terminals of the first ceiling rose in the circuit. From this ceiling rose the cable loops out to the next, then the next, and so on until all the ceiling roses or lighting points have been linked together. A length of the same cable runs from each loop-in ceiling rose to the switch controlling the light.

The joint box system

The same type of cable is used, starting at a 5A fuse in the consumer unit or fuse board. It runs to a series of joint boxes instead of direct to the ceiling roses or lighting point. It is usually necessary to have one joint box for each light and its switch (Fig. 15). From

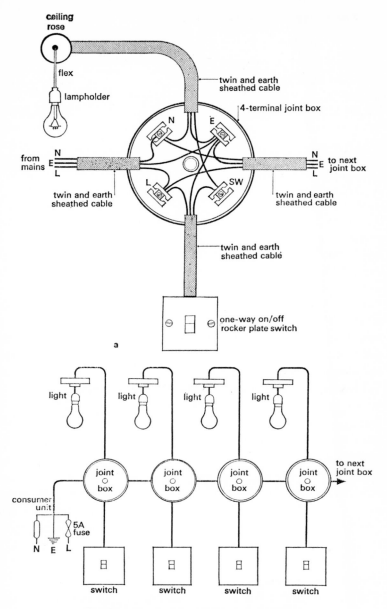

ceiling
rose

flex

lampholder

twin and earth
sheathed cable

4-terminal joint box

N E

from
mains

N
E
L

to next
joint box

N
E
L

L SW

twin and earth
sheathed cable

twin and earth
sheathed cable

twin and earth
sheathed cable

one-way on/off
rocker plate switch

a

light   light   light   light

joint
box   joint
box   joint
box   joint
box

to next
joint box

consumer
unit

5A
fuse

N E L

switch   switch   switch   switch

all cables 1.0 sq mm twin and earth P.V.C. sheathed

b

Fig. 15   Wiring a lighting circuit: joint box system (a) joint box
connections (b) general circuit layout

each joint box run two similar cables; one to the switch and the other to the lighting point.

Circular in shape each joint box has four terminals: the live 'L' the neutral 'N'; the switch return wire 'SW' and the earth 'E'. Connections are made as in Fig 15a. When more than one light is controlled by the same switch (such as wall lights) one joint box is used for all the lights but a separate cable is run from it to each light.

TWO-WAY SWITCHING

This controls one light from two different switch positions, for example: a light on the staircase can have one switch on the landing and another in the hall; a bedroom light can be controlled by one switch on the wall near the door and another at the bedhead, usually a cord operated ceiling switch.

There are a number of ways of wiring this. The usual and best method for a sheathed cable system is to wire the light as for a 1-way switch, using a twin-core and earth cable, and to link the two switches by a 3-core and earth cable (Fig. 17a). Both switches are 2-way.

This method can also be used to convert an existing 1-way switch to a 2-way circuit. The 1-way switch is replaced by a 2-way, a length of 3-core and earth pvc sheathed cable is run from the switch to the second switch position and the connections are made (Fig. 17a).

Fig. 16   Switching circuits for lighting (a) one-way switch connections

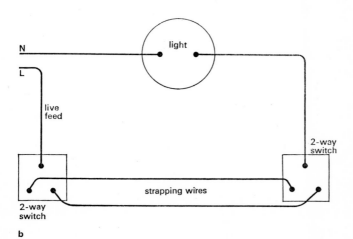

Fig. 17 Switching circuits for lighting (a) 2-way switch connections
(b) conventional 2-way switch circuit

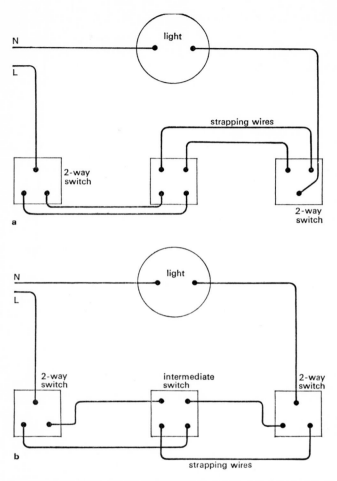

Fig. 18 Switching circuits for lighting (a) intermediate switch
connections (b) alternative connections

The conventional 2-way switching circuit is shown in Fig. 17b.
With this method a live conductor is run to the 'common' terminal
of one of the 2-way switches, a switch return wire runs from the
'common' terminal of the other 2-way switch to the light, and the
two are linked by a twin-core (and earth) cable termed the *strapping*

wires. This is used in conduit systems but rarely in sheathed cable systems.

INTERMEDIATE SWITCHING CIRCUITS

This circuit enables a light to be switched on and off from three or more different positions. Basically it is a 2-way switching circuit using two 2-way switches, one at each end of the circuit, linked by strapping wires, one for each additional switch position required. These are outwardly identical to 1- and 2-way switches but have four terminals. There are two types each having different internal connections. The circuits giving the external connections are shown in Figs 18a & b.

Cord-operated ceiling switches are also used for 2-way and intermediate switching circuits. There is no intermediate ceiling switch so the ceiling switch must be one or other of the 2-way switch positions of an intermediate switching circuit.

DIMMER SWITCH CONTROL

Any light fitting which uses tungsten filament lamps can be controlled by one of the new dimmer switches. These are electronic devices which include a component termed a *thyrister*—type of transistor—and a printed circuit. No special circuit wiring is required and it is fitted in place of an on/off switch to vary the light from full brilliance down to off. The dimmer switch fits the standard pattress box used for mounting plate switches and versions of it are available for fluorescent lights.

When used in a 2-way or in an intermediate switching circuit the dimmer switch is often additional and the other switches operate the light without affecting the setting of the dimmer. This arrangement can be useful in a bedroom or on the landing. Some makes of dimmer switch will replace the 2-way switch itself.

One version of the dimmer includes an on/off switch which enables the light to be switched to full brilliance temporarily without altering the dimmer setting. This is useful during breaks in the television programme or when attending to a child in bed or a sick member of the family.

F

ADDING A LIGHT

This can be done very simply by running a twin-core and earth pvc sheathed cable from the flex terminals of a ceiling rose to the new light. Both lights are then controlled by the one switch but cannot be switched on and off independently. If independent switching is wanted then it is necessary to locate a source of current—a live feed terminal for the switch and a neutral feed for the light—either in a joint box or a loop-in ceiling rose.

From these terminals, and the earth terminal, a 1 sq. mm twin-core and earth cable is run to a new joint box fixed roughly midway between the new light and switch. From there a length of similar cable is run to the new light and another length is run down the wall to the switch. Alternatively the feed cable can be run directly to a loop-in ceiling rose so dispensing with a joint box, and from this a cable run to the switch. (A cord-operated ceiling switch will save running a cable down a wall.)

ADDING WALL LIGHTS

Wall lights can be the main lighting in a room or they can supplement that from a ceiling pendant. They can be independently controlled by a separate switch and each wall light can be individually controlled by its own integral switch. (Not all wall lights have integral switches; many are unswitched.) Alternatively, switched wall lights can be wired from the existing ceiling light and be turned on and off with it, or individually when only the pendant light is needed. This saves running a new cable down to a wall switch. Whichever method is used the principal job is to run the cables from under the floorboards in the room above, down to the wall lights below.

A more simple type to install are the pin-up ones, which are fed by flexible cord from plugs and socket-outlets situated adjacent to or immediately below the fitting. Wall lights may also be supplied from fixed wiring connected to a ring circuit via a fused connection unit.

REPLACING A CEILING ROSE

Old ceiling roses can, to advantage, be replaced by the new loop-in type irrespective of the method of wiring (loop-in or joint box system) but the connections are slightly different.

Ceiling roses with three terminals (3-plate ceiling roses) are used with loop-in systems and those with two terminals (2-plate ceiling roses) are used with joint box systems. In practice you may find this to be the reverse: in the first case one of the three terminals will be blank; in the second case the necessary live cable connection or joint has been made above the ceiling rose, sometimes in the terminals of a pattress box. The new ceiling rose will rectify any discrepancy for it has three sets of terminals plus an earth terminal (see photographs).

The three sets or rows of terminals are *Live*, usually in the centre, flanked by *neutral* and *switch wire*. The outer two contain terminal connections for the flexible cord conductors and are usually marked 'flex'! The live terminal has no flex connection and is shrouded in accordance with regulations to prevent a person touching it.

When removing an old ceiling rose first examine the terminal connections which are exposed on unscrewing the cover. If it is a 3-plate type only two of the terminals will carry the flex and these must be noted. If the third terminal contains circuit conductors, as it will with a loop-in system, these are the live conductors and must be connected to the live terminals of the new ceiling rose. If the third terminal is blank, there is no connection problem for there will only be two sets of conductors to deal with. If the ceiling rose is of the 2-plate type the flex will be connected to both, one core to each, but on removing the ceiling rose check that there are no jointed conductors behind it or behind the mounting block.

Disconnect the cables from the old ceiling rose taking care not to allow individual conductors to come apart from their joints. To prevent a mix-up, take the live conductors off first and wrap the ends in a piece of red pvc adhesive tape. The two remaining groups of conductors, or the sole two from a 2-plate ceiling rose, have to be identified before they can be connected to the new rose. One is the neutral and will usually have two or more conductors which should all have black insulation. The other is usually a single conductor, being the switch wire, and should have red insulation or a red sleeve but this wire is often black too.

If both are single conductors, one red and one black, the black is the neutral and the red the switch wire and should be connected to the new ceiling rose in the normal way. If both are black, as they will be if it is the last lighting point of a circuit wired on the loop-in system, it will be necessary to ascertain which is the live switch wire and which is the neutral. With the mains and the light switch on, test the conductors by touching them with a neon tester (screwdriver): the conductor which causes the neon to glow is the switch wire. As a final check, turn off the light switch and apply the neon tester again to the conductor. This time the neon should not glow. *Don't forget to turn off the mains switch before continuing the job.*

Some old roses, usually plastic types, are fixed direct to the ceiling whereas others, especially when made of porcelain, are mounted on circular wood blocks. If there is a wood block remove it and fix the new rose direct to the ceiling, but take care not to disturb the conductor joints.

Now remove the thin plastic knockout in the centre of the base of the new ceiling rose and thread in the cables, making sure that

Fig. 19   Fixing a ceiling light

the sheathing terminates within the rose. Fix the rose with wood screws to a joist or a piece of timber fixed between two joints. (Use a piece of timber $3 \times \frac{3}{4}$ in. thick (75×20 mm) and drill a $\frac{3}{4}$ in. (20 mm) hole to take the cables.) A ceiling rose or a light fitting must not rely on laths of a lath and plaster ceiling for its sole support.

The conductors are then connected to the terminals of the ceiling rose. One conductor is inserted in each terminal hole of the modern ceiling rose which means that jointed conductors are now released taking one joint at a time to avoid mixing up the conductors. As the old lighting circuit has no earth conductor the earth terminal remains blank. The flex and the lampholder are then fixed to the ceiling rose.

FITTING A NEW WALL SWITCH

The old surface mounted tumbler switch on a wood block is now obsolete and has been replaced by the modern plate switch having a rocker, and with some patterns, a dolly. These switches are mounted on moulded plastic surface pattress boxes or metal boxes which are sunk into the wall flush with the plaster. As the switches are interchangeable you can mount them first on surface boxes and later, when re-decorating, fit them to flush boxes.

The surface plate of the switch is usually $3\frac{1}{8}$ in. square and is made in one- two- and three-gang switch versions, each gang comprising an independently operated switch. The one-gang switch has variations too: one-way; 2-way; intermediate: double-pole; and some special types. For most situations a one-way is used; for 2-way switching a 2-way version is used. All the switches of the two- and three-gang versions are 2-way. Any 2-way switch can be used as a one-way on/off switch. When a two-gang switch is used as the two switches in the one position, either or both can be used as one-way switches. For example in the hall, one switch is used as a one-way switch for the hall light and the other is used as a 2-way switch for the landing light. An intermediate switch is available only as one-gang and must be mounted separately from others.

Fig. 20   Fixing a lighting switch to a surface box

Switches and moulded surface pattress boxes are made in various tones of white and ivory; also in brown and their plates differ slightly in style between makes.

REPLACING A TUMBLER SWITCH

Remove the old switch and its wood block from the wall, taking care not to damage the conductors. If the new switch is to be surface mounted, select the surface box and remove the thin plastic to receive the cable. Thread on the cable making sure the sheath enters the box. Fix the box by wood screws into plugged holes. Connect the ends of the two conductors to the two terminals and secure the switch to the box by the two screws (4BA or M3·5 if metric) provided with the switch.

If, on examination, the insulation at the ends of the conductors is worn they should be enclosed in red pvc sleeving. Or, if the cable down to the switch is run in conduit it may, after checking that there is enough slack about the ceiling, be possible to pull a few inches through and cut off the worn end. Brittle insulation indicates the need for an early re-wire.

Fitting a metal flush box is a little more complicated. The flush box for the plates, which is of plaster with a rubber or pvc grommet in the top for the sheathed cable entry has to be pierced to take the cable.

After removing the old tumbler switch and block remove the bits of plaster around the cable and check whether the cable of the switch drop is run in conduit. If it is, the flush box will have to be fixed below the end of the conduit, but first fit a rubber bush on the end of metal conduit if there is not one already. If the switch will be too low in that position you can either fit a surface box, or,

Fig. 21 Fixing a lighting switch to a flush box

if the conduit is plastic you may be able to cut the conduit *in situ* taking care not to damage the cable. It is possible to shorten steel conduit *in situ* if you can first withdraw the cable. It is a difficult job but usually worth the trouble.

To fit the box: place it in position on the wall and run a pencil around the edge. Chop out the plaster using an old wide-blade wood chisel or a sharp cold chisel. Place the box in the chase. If it is not flush with the plaster surface remove sufficient brick-work to give more depth. Thread the cable through the grommet and ensure that the end of the sheath enters the box. Fix the box with wood screws in plugged holes, but before tightening them level the box by means of the slotted screw hole. Connect the conductors to the switch terminals and fix the switch with the screws provided.

If the insulation of the conductors is worn or brittle enclose them in red pvc sleeving as for the surface boxes.

Modern patterns of surface and flush switch boxes have an earth terminal for the earth continuity conductor of the circuit.

Where there is not one, as with most existing lighting circuits, this terminal remains blank until the circuit is rewired with cable containing an earth conductor.

There are also metal plate switches in a variety of finishes. When these are fitted it is necessary to earth each plate by running a conductor to each switch. The cable can be a green pvc insulated conductor run from the consumer unit. Where the switch drop cable is run in conduit it is usually possible to pass the cable down the conduit alongside the existing cable. Otherwise, the cable has to be run separately or a plastic switch fitted instead.

It is not possible to fit a flush box to a lath and plaster partition nor to a dry partition wall except by chopping out some lath and plaster and inserting a support for the box or by using a special box (in a dry partition wall) but you must be prepared for a tricky job.

RUNNING AND FIXING CABLES
When installing electric wiring in the house there are a number

of details which must be observed to ensure that the work will comply with the IEE Wiring Regulations.

If cables are run under the floor that which crosses floor joists

Fig. 22 Running indoor cables (a) threading cable through joists (b) fishing a cable under floorboards

must be threaded through holes drilled at least 2 in. (50 mm) below the tops of the joists. Alternatively it may be run in slots cut in the tops of joists but it must be protected from possible damage when floorboards are nailed. If slots already exist, such as when a house is rewired, they can only be used if protected by metal joist inserts made for the purpose.

When cables are run through the roof these are not normally threaded through holes in the joists unless the loft is to be boarded or used as storage space. Instead they are fixed to the tops of joists where they remain undisturbed. In the vicinity of the cold water storage tank, which must have access to it, cables are likely to get damaged and are therefore not fixed to the tops of joists.

Cables laid under floorboards at ground level of a house, or under the floor of a bungalow, need be fixed only where they are likely to be disturbed. Normally they are laid on the concrete and require no additional support.

SURFACE CABLES

Cables run on the surface of walls and ceilings must be properly fixed using the correct clips. There are various types of clips, but the modern and most simple to use is the expanded pvc clip which is fixed by a carbon steel pin supplied with each. They range in size for all types of house wiring sheathed cable.

Maximum distances between clips are specified in the regulations. For general house wiring sheathed cables these are: 9 in. (225 mm) for horizontal runs and 15 in. (400 mm) for vertical runs. But to eliminate any risk of sagging it is better to reduce the spacings: 6 in. (150 mm) horizontal, 9 in. (225 mm) vertical.

Fixing a cable in a straight line is important but not always easy, and the best way to do it is to first mark a pencil line with a straight edge or, you can use a length of chalked string and 'snap' a line between the two points.

SINKING CABLES IN WALLS

Because pvc sheathed cables are expected to last the life of the building they may be buried in chases cut in the wall and plastered over without the use of conduit or other additional protection. Also, conduit or casing does not protect a cable from drills or plugging tools. But if you are likely to remove the cable down to switches or wall lights at a future date, it should be enclosed in conduit so that you can withdraw it without disturbing the wall plaster.

Non-sheathed insulated pvc cable must be enclosed in conduit or trunking throughout its length and *must not* be used for ordinary house wiring jobs except in an all-conduit installation or circuit. The only exception is a green pvc insulated non-sheathed cable used for earthing purposes.

CONDUIT INSTALLATION
Before the last war some houses were wired in light gauge metal conduit complete with metal elbows, tees, and other fittings. These are now usually rewired with pvc sheathed cable and most of the conduit removed or abandoned. At switch drops and similar positions the conduit may be used to carry the new cable but rubber or pvc bushes must be fitted to the ends of such conduit.

Extensions to a conduit installation, such as new lights and other extras, may be run in pvc sheathed cable without conduit and treated as a normal pvc sheathed installation.

TRUNKING
Where floors are solid it is necessary to make alternative arrangements. It is in these situations that cable trunking becomes useful if not essential, be it a bungalow, a flat or the ground floor of the conventional 2-storey house.

The trunking can be fixed above the skirting board but it is sometimes possible to replace the wooden skirting by plastic trunking with skirting profile.

In the older house with deep skirtings the narrower modern skirting will not fill the gap left if the old is removed. In this case it is possible to fix the plastic trunking to the existing skirting board. Some trunking incorporates socket-outlets which may be inserted in any position. With other types you can use Crabtree multi-purpose pattresses made in single- and two-gang versions for single and double socket-outlets and other wiring accessories.

EARTH CONTINUITY CONDUCTORS (ECC)

Every circuit of an installation must have an earth continuity conductor termed the ecc. In sheathed cable wiring the ecc as already stated is the non-insulated conductor situated between the two that are insulated. In metal conduit wiring the conduit itself is used as the ecc. In plastic conduit wiring a green insulated conductor is used for the ecc; and also in plastic trunking, except where sheathed cables containing an ecc are used.

With mineral insulated copper cables (MICC cable) and wire armour cables used in outdoor wiring, the metal sheath or the wire armour is the ecc.

For most house wiring work the ecc is enclosed in the sheathing of the cable. As the ends of the ecc are bare when the sheath of the cable is removed for making the connections at the terminals it is necessary to enclose them in green pvc sleeving.

Their purpose is to earth the metalwork of fittings and appliances and connections are provided in ceiling roses and in switch boxes for terminating the earth cable. Where the switch, like the usual ceiling rose, is insulated and earthing is not needed, the ecc is still at the terminal for use if metal switches are fitted later.

The ecc of power circuits is connected direct to the earth terminal of the socket-outlet, fused connection unit, or cord outlet unit. Some metal boxes used with socket-outlets and other power accessories have an earthing terminal which is used to connect the accessory to earth when the installation is wired in metal conduit, and there is no separate earth wire. If you buy a box with an earth terminal do not use this terminal with pvc sheathed cable containing an ecc.

Although every circuit must now have an ecc running throughout it, only since 1967 has one had to be included in a lighting circuit. Most lighting circuits still have no ecc though it is necessary to run one where metal switches are used or lighting fittings have exposed metalwork. Earthing is particularly important with metal wall lights for these can be touched by a person standing on the floor.

LIFTING FLOORBOARDS

When it is necessary to raise floorboards to run the cables underneath you should first look for any which have been raised previously because they will be easier to lift. Tools you need are: a 2½ lb hammer; two electrician's bolster chisels; a cold chisel at least 12 in. (300 mm) long; a nail punch; a tenon saw and a rip saw. A padsaw is also useful.

When a board is lifted for the first time try to select one which is butt-jointed to another and does not extend the full length of the room. Insert a bolster chisel at each edge of the board and lever up the end. Place the cold chisel under the raised end of the board with its ends resting on the adjacent boards. Ease the board up further along its length using the two bolster chisels. Then lift the end of the board and roll the cold chisel along as far as it will go. Release the board and apply a downward pressure on the end. With the cold chisel acting as a fulcrum the remainder of the board will be prised up and with it the fixing nails. This process is repeated until the complete board is lifted and can be

Fig. 23   Lifting floorboards (a) prising floorboard with bolster chisels
(b) using cold chisel to hold raised end of floorboard

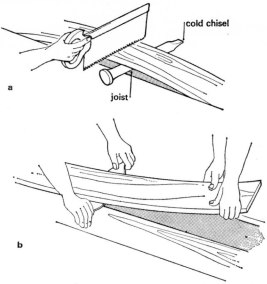

Fig. 24   (a) Cutting a floorboard (b) prising floorboard with cold chisel

wrenched out of the joist under the skirting. Now knock out the nails in the board and extract the others from the joists.

Where a board has no join it will be necessary to cut it at a suitable position. To do this the board must be raised at this point by punching in the nails in three joists including the joist where the cut is being made. Then using the two bolster chisels lift the board at the joist and insert the cold chisel underneath near the joist. Using the tenon saw cut the board at a point coinciding with the centre of the joist so that when relaid, both sections of the board will be supported by it. When the board has been cut, the required section or both halves can be lifted in the manner just described.

For T & G (tongued and grooved) boards it is necessary first to cut off the tongue on each side of the board (one being the tongue of the adjacent board). This is done with the rip saw but it is essential to ensure you are not cutting cables or damaging hot and cold water pipes. When the tongues have been ripped off the lifting procedure is as before.

REPLACING BOARDS

When replacing floorboards check there are no bent nails or other obstructions to prevent the board seating properly. Make certain that a board is replaced the right way round and that jointed boards butt each other. Floorboards can be refixed with oval brads (2 in. oval nails) but where covering a joint box and above light fittings, screw them down so that they can readily be raised if necessary. The board above a lighting point need only be a trap extending over two joists, before fixing these traps insert timber between the joists for securing light fittings.

Boards usually butt against the wall and therefore extend under the skirting board. When a cable passes up the wall from the joist to feed socket-outlets fixed above the skirting this cable, or cables, will foul the board and could be damaged. To prevent this cut a nick in the end of the floorboard as a channel for the cables.

CABLES BURIED IN THE WALL

I have already said that pvc sheathed cables may be buried in the plaster of a wall and as such needs no further protection. The ordinary flat twin and 3-core sheathed cable can usually be accommodated in a plaster depth chase, but where the plaster is thin it will be necessary to cut into the brickwork or breeze. The chase can be made good with a plaster filler and papered over or painted. Cables should be chased when re-decorating the room. No chasing is necessary in lath and plaster partitions or in cavity walls for the cable can be run down the cavity to a hole drilled in the wall at the outlet or switch position.

When running cables down the cavity of lath and plaster partitions, cross members of timber may obstruct them. Such cross members have to be drilled to take the cable. For drilling a long auger is necessary.

When cables are to be run in conduit down to the switches the oval type of pvc conduit should be used to reduce the amount of chasing required.

COVERING CABLES

Cables run on the surface may be covered in capping made of wood, plastic or metal for a neater job. An alternative method of surface wiring is to run cables in plastic trunking. This is mainly used for wiring ring circuits, using trunking of the skirting type, but it is also used for the lighting circuit wiring the trunking being of the mini-type including architrave trunking at switch drops.

TABLE 5

Circuit cables pvc sheathed

Circuit	*Fuse Wire*	*Cable size (metric)*	*Cable (metric) Current rating*	*Cable size (imperial)*
	amps	mm²	amps	No. and diam. of wires
Lighting	5	1·0 or 1·5	12 or 15	1/·044 or 3/·029
Immersion heater	15 (or 20)	2·5	21	7/·029
Ring circuit and spurs	30	2·5	21	7/·029
Radial circuit (20A)	20	2·5	21	7/.029
Radial circuit (30A)	30	4	27	7/.036
Cooker (family size)	45	6 or 10	35 or 48	7/·044 or 7/·052
Meter tails		10 or 16	48 or 64	7/.064 or 19/.044

NB. The cable current ratings shown, are when the fuses are the fusewire rewirable type. These current ratings can be uprated by one-third if cartridge fuses or mcb's are fitted in the consumer unit.

12 | The Ring Circuit

The domestic ring circuit is a comparatively recent development and was designed to enable a large number of portable electrical appliances and certain stationary appliances, not exceeding 3kW each, to be run off the one circuit with little if any risk of overloading.

The circuit has a current rating of 30A and each individual appliance is supplied from it via a 13A fused outlet. This is usually a plug and socket but for a stationary appliance it may be a fused connection unit, also known as a *fused spur box*.

Any number of 13A socket-outlets and fused spur boxes may be fed from one ring circuit but the area supplied must not be greater than 1080 sq. ft (100 sq. metres). Where the floor area exceeds this, additional ring circuits have to be installed at the rate of one for each 100 sq. metres or part thereof. This restriction limits the likely load on the ring circuit, for obviously, the larger the area supplied the greater the potential load. (Adding outlets to a ring circuit does not increase the load demand.)

A stationary electrical appliance is one fixed to the wall, ceiling or floor, such as a wall heater; or built-in or free standing, such as a refrigerator; the load in each case must not exceed 3kW. Electric clocks also come within this category, whether mounted wall or table clocks and are supplied from special fused clock connector units. Shaver supply units (shaver sockets) may be connected to the ring circuit too. (There are two types of shaver socket: one has a transformer and is installed in the bathroom; the other kind is much cheaper, has no transformer, and may be installed in any room except the bathroom.) It is regarded as good practice to instal two ring circuits in the 2–3 bedroom house even where the floor area is within 100 sq. metres. One supplies the ground floor and the other the first floor. Two circuits should

G

wall panel heater

switched fused spur box with flex outlet and neon indicator

flex

.clock

flex

fused clock connector

double socket-outlet

to lights

spur cable

30A joint box

fused spur box

3A fu

double socket outlet

single socket outlet

neutral link   30A circuit fuse

earth

Fig. 25   Typical ring circuit

also be installed in the conventional bungalow with the outlets fairly evenly distributed between the two.

Lighting points, although normally supplied from 5A lighting circuits, may within limits be supplied from a ring circuit.

WIRING THE RING CIRCUIT

This circuit has a current rating of 30A supplied from a 30A fuseway or miniature circuit breaker of a consumer unit. The cable used is 2·5 sq. mm twin and earth sheathed, wired to form a ring which starts and ends at the terminals of the fuseway.

Socket-outlets or fused connection units for stationary appliances may be connected at any point along the ring. Although this circuit has a current rating of 30A the cable is only rated at about 20A, because each outlet is fed by two cables—the outward and the return.

In addition, others may be fed from spurs branching off the ring cable, to supply outlets in remote positions. The number of spurs which may be connected is restricted to the number of socket-outlets and fixed appliances connected to the ring cable: if there are say eight outlets, eight extra spurs may be wired.

Any one spur may supply not more than two single socket-outlets, or one double socket-outlet, or one fixed appliance. A ring circuit with eight socket-outlets on it may have eight spurs each supplying two socket-outlets making a total of sixteen, plus eight on the ring cable which is a grand total of twenty-four. In practice there will normally be fewer spurs than permitted in the regulations.

Spur cables are the same size and type as used to wire the ring. They may be connected to the ring cable either at 30A 3-terminal ring circuit joint boxes or at the terminals of socket-outlets and fused spur boxes (fused connection units). When looping a spur cable out of a joint box it is best not to cut the ring cable. Instead, remove the required amount of sheath and insulation, lay the bared conductors into the terminals with the ends alongside the ring conductors and tighten the terminals. As the earth conductor is not insulated do this with green pvc insulation tape.

When adding a spur cable to the terminals of a ring socket-outlet or fused connection unit, place them by the sides of the existing conductors and tighten the terminals. As the 2·5 sq. mm cable is a solid single-strand conductor it is not possible to twist the ends in the form of a joint. Also, do not attempt to insert more conductors than the capacity of the terminals. Only one spur can be connected to any one joint box or socket-outlet so do not try to exceed this.

FUSED SPURS

The ordinary spur, as we have seen, is solidly connected to the ring cable at the joint box or socket-outlet. Others, known as *fused spurs*, may be run from the 'LOAD' or 'OUT' terminals of a fused spur box. As such these are protected individually by the spur fuse and may supply a number of outlets having a total capacity of 13A or less.

Wall lights can be supplied from a fused spur as can a bathroom heat/light unit or heater where no socket-outlet or switch is permitted if within reach of a person using the bath or shower.

The 13A socket-outlet fitted to ring circuits and spurs is made in a variety of types: single-, double-, and three-gang. There are switched and non-switched versions, and switched versions with neon indicators. Most types can be fitted on to metal boxes sunk flush into the wall or they can be fitted to surface boxes. Some patterns are designed for surface mounting only. All 13A plugs have fuses but some versions are switched and have a neon indicator (so do some non-switched 13A fused plugs).

FIXED HEIGHTS

The recommended fixing height of a socket-outlet should be not less than 6 in. (150 mm) above the level of the floor or a working surface such as in the kitchen.

However, it is more convenient for old or disabled people to have sockets situated higher on the wall, say at one metre above the floor level. This saves them having to stoop to withdraw the plug or switch off the socket. Where young children are concerned it is better to keep the sockets nearer the floor to avoid trailing flexes which can cause accidents.

RADIAL POWER CIRCUITS

Radial power circuits, or radial final sub-circuits to give them their official name, are multi-outlet circuits in two current ratings—20A and 30A—supplying either a maximum of two or a maximum of six 13A socket-outlets or fixed appliances.

A 20A radial circuit is wired in 2·5 sq. mm twin and earth sheathed and it may supply up to a maximum of two 13A socket-outlets, which can be in different parts of the house. The same circuit may also supply up to a maximum of six socket-outlets (except a water heater) and fixed appliances if they are all in one room (other than a kitchen) and the room has a floor area of less than 300 sq. ft or 30 m². Either of these circuits is supplied from a 20A fuse in the consumer unit.

The 20A two-outlet version has many applications where two additional points are needed and there is no ring circuit. The 6-outlet version is suitable for the average bedroom or sitting room instead of a ring circuit or supplementing an existing one. It can be installed in the bed-sitter within its limitations and can be separately metered by a checkmeter or slot meter. It is also suitable for the garage or workshop.

The 30A six-outlet radial circuit is wired in 4 sq. mm twin-core and earth pvc sheathed cable originating at a 30A fuse in the consumer unit. It has a wide range of applications, and provided no more than six outlets are required it can be used as an alternative to a ring circuit. Especially suitable for the kitchen it may supply a fixed water heater at the sink in addition to five other outlets. It is also suitable for the bed-sitter where a fixed water heater is required and not permitted from the 20A version. Another application is the garage or workshop detached from the house where above average power is required, or for the heated greenhouse.

Either the 20A or the 30A radial circuit can be converted into a ring circuit by running a return cable back to the fuse unit. Additional outlets can then be fixed as for any ring circuit.

13 | Outdoor Wiring

Electricity can be used satisfactorily and with safety outside the house provided the work is carried out correctly using the proper cables and equipment. For most householders outdoor wiring consists of running a cable to a detached garage, workshop, shed or greenhouse. But when electricity is required to power a fountain, a pump in the pool or garden lighting; or to supply an electric mower, hedge trimmer or other electrical garden tools, points usually need to be fixed outside to eliminate trailing flexes from the house. Outside lights attached to the house and the switches which control them also need to be wired properly.

ELECTRICITY TO OUTDOOR BUILDINGS
A detached building, even if it is only a few feet away from the house, has to be treated as a separate building requiring a supply of electricity independent from that of the house. Regulations do not now permit such a supply to be extended from any circuit in the house. This applies to a garage or a greenhouse, whether it be fitted with a substantial amount of electrical equipment, or just one light.

The requirements for running a supply to another building are: (i) a special cable running from the mains supply in the house, (ii) a main switch and fuse unit in the house; and (iii) an isolating switch and fuse unit in the outbuilding. The outdoor cable may be run overhead, underground or along a wall. *Under no circumstances may a cable of any sort be run along the garden fence.* The type of cable used depends on the method, and to some extent on the distance between house and outbuilding.

Overhead method
For this you can use ordinary sheathed house wiring cable sus-

Fig. 26 Running an outdoor cable overhead

pended from, or attached to, a catenary wire strained between the house and outbuilding. If the span between the house and garage or shed is not more than 10 ft (3 m) you may dispense with the catenary and run the cable without any additional support. For this distance too the cable may be run in an unjointed length of steel conduit. The minimum height above the general ground level for the cable alone is 12 ft (3.5 m) and where contained in conduit it is 10 ft (3 m).

For longer spans, where supported by a catenary, the cable at its lowest point must not be less than 12ft (3·5 m) above the general ground level or 17 ft (5.2 m) if there is access for vehicles beneath it.

The catenary is fixed by an eye bolt or other suitable fastening at one end, and to a straining eye bolt at the other. For very long runs down the garden an overhead cable needs intermediate supports, usually poles.

The cable is either fixed to the catenary by insulation tape and clips or is suspended from it by special rawhide or plastic slings.

The catenary cable must be bonded to earth but not used as the circuit earth continuity conductor. This is contained within the cable itself.

Underground method
A cable laid underground between the house and outbuilding must be buried at least 18 in. (500 mm) below the surface of the ground. Preferably route the trench where the ground is unlikely to be disturbed in the future, the edge of a lawn or pathway is usually satisfactory. If the cable has to cross a vegetable plot or other places where deep digging is likely, a trench deeper than 18 in. (500 mm) is advised. Additional protection of the cable such as covering it with linked cable tiles is normally unnecessary.

Fig. 27   Running an outdoor cable underground

Two cables recommended for running underground which may be buried direct in the soil are: (i) armoured cable which has an overall extruded pvc sheath—usually black; and (ii) mineral insulated metal sheathed (MICC) cable which has an overall extruded covering of pvc, usually orange in colour. This covering is to protect the galvanised steel wire armour of the armoured cable, or the copper sheath of the mineral insulated cable, from the corrosive effect of the soil. The cable is twin core of the appropriate size and current rating for the circuit; the wire armour or the copper sheath being used as the earth continuity conductor.

An alternative underground system is twin-core and earth pvc sheathed cable run in conduit. The conduit must be either heavy gauge galvanised steel, which is preferred, or rigid pvc. Where high impact plastic conduit is used it must not be exposed to ambient temperatures below $-5°C$ because it is apt to fracture. Steel conduit must be bonded to earth but must not be used as the circuit earth continuity conductor.

TERMINATING AND JOINTING UNDERGROUND CABLE
Mineral insulated cable must have a seal fitted at each end to keep out the moisture for the insulation is hygroscopic. Fitting seals is a fairly difficult job requiring special tools and materials but the cable can be bought in cut lengths already fitted with the seals. When the cable is terminated in a metal junction box or into a screwed outlet of a fitting or wiring accessory it requires a screwed gland. The glands are fitted at the same time as the seals, so it is better to buy the cable with both seals and glands fitted.

Armoured cable also requires a gland at each end to contain the wire armour and to ensure a good electrical connection for the earthing in the junction box or accessory. Where the supply position in the house or the isolating switch in the outbuilding is some distance from the point of entry of the underground cable, it is better to terminate the underground cable in a junction box and run the remainder of it in ordinary twin-core and earth house wiring cable. The junction box to use is the metal knockout type used for mounting socket-outlets flush with the wall. The two ¾ in. (20 mm) blanks are removed from the box sides. These accept the glands of the cable which are secured by brass screwed bushes or steel conduit locknuts, but first the edges of the holes must be cleaned of enamel to ensure good earth connection and continuity. The boxes are fitted with blanking-off plates which serve as covers.

Where cable is run in conduit for the underground section of the outdoor circuit no junction boxes are needed as this cable runs direct to the switches in house and outbuilding. The conduit is terminated at the point of entry in the building. If steel conduit is used it is fitted with a rubber bush to protect the cable sheath.

Choosing the right type of cable

Armoured twin and earth cable is the best for underground purposes. It is easy to handle and as pvc insulation is non-hygroscopic no sealing of the ends is required. Also for its current rating it is less subject to voltage drop when loaded to capacity.

The next best choice is mineral insulated copper sheathed cable. This has the advantage of being smaller in diameter in sections where it runs on the surface. It can normally enter the house via an air vent above the damp course except if bought fitted with seals when it will not pass through a vent hole.

Conduit, the third choice, is more difficult to install. If of steel, threads have to be cut for jointing which needs stocks and dies—not normally part of a householder's tool kit. Plastic conduit is fairly easy to install and the cable requires no seals or glands because it is ordinary sheathed.

Surface method

Only where there is a wall extending down the garden, or for most of the run, is this method possible for under *no circumstances may cable be fixed to a fence*. Cable is, however, frequently run on the exterior wall of the house to feed outside lights and switches.

The best cable to use in this situation is mineral insulated copper sheathed having an extruded pvc covering of orange colour. Armoured cable and also heavy gauge galvanised steel conduit may also be fixed to and run along an outside wall but both are unsightly. Where appearance is unimportant armoured can be used.

Outdoor sections of cable which feed an outside light or switch fixed to a wall of the house or garage must also be mineral insulated, or armoured cable, or cable run in conduit (even where the outdoor section is only a few inches). It is often possible to run the cable inside the house or building and pass it through the wall immediately behind the outside light or switch. This may mean altering the chosen positions of the light (or switch) but it is worth it to save the outdoor run.

Cable run along outside walls is secured by clips, fixed at the same maximum distances as for inside runs: 15 in. (400 mm) apart for vertical runs and 9 in. (250 mm) for horizontal runs.

OUTDOOR CABLE SIZES

Cables supplying an outside garage, workshop, shed or green-house must be of adequate size to carrry the load and to ensure there is no significant voltage drop on long runs.

A cable which feeds just a light in a shed a few feet from the house need not be more than 1.5 sq. mm run from a 5A fuseway in the house. For most situations where there is likely to be other equipment used, the minimum size is 2·5 sq. mm from a 20A fuseway, this being a 20A radial circuit. For long runs of 50 ft or more and where heating is to be installed you should install a 30A circuit using 4 sq. mm cable. A 30A circuit using 4 sq. mm cable should be run to a heated greenhouse.

Cable running to an outside light or switch fixed to the house or other building need to be only 1·5 sq. mm size, but for socket-outlets in the garden 2·5 sq. mm size cable must be used where these are of the 13A fused plug type. Mineral insulated cable is buried in the soil in the same way as running a cable to an outside building. The socket-outlets should be fixed to a garden wall or to stout posts, at a height of not less than 6 in. (150 mm) above ground level. Weatherproof socket-outlets are used, which may be metal clad or unbreakable rubber fitted with hinged covers.

14 | Electric Bells, Buzzers and Chimes

The ordinary domestic electric bell usually operates at the low voltage of between $4\frac{1}{2}$V and 8V. It is called the trembler bell because of the trembling action of the electro-magnet and contact system. It operates equally well on DC from a battery as on AC from a mains transformer. Some domestic bells, as with their commercial counterparts, operate on AC only and have a different contact system to that of the trembler bell. If an AC bell is connected to a battery it will only produce a single strike each time the push is operated and the circuit closed.

A buzzer is constructed similarly to a trembler bell, or an AC bell, but has neither striker nor gong. The contacts, which have only a small gap between them, produce a high note which has been compared to the wings of a bee in flight—hence the name.

A bell circuit, also used to supply a buzzer, is very simple and as the bell operates at extra low voltage (elv), below 50 volts, the wire used is only lightly insulated and is known as bell wire. The battery or transformer to supply the circuit can be situated in any convenient position and in some models it is contained in the bell casing itself.

Twin (2-core) bell wire is normally used for the circuit, it being much neater, when run on the surface, than single wire. One length of twin bell wire is run from the battery or transformer to the bell; another length runs from the bell to its push. As it is twin wire a joint has to be made in one of the conductors at the bell. The wire is fixed with insulated bell staples, or alternatively self-adhesive wire is available.

The bell push, fitted at the front door, is made in a variety of styles and types including illuminated versions which contain a small torch bulb. An illuminated push is possible only when the

Fig. 28   Interior view of trembler bell showing connections and
contacts

bell, buzzer or chimes are powered from a mains transformer,
the bulb which is alight continuously, i.e. except for the moment
when the push is being operated, would drain the battery within a
day. The bulb, within its push, is connected across the two terminals of the push and is in effect wired in series with the bell.
It does, in fact, provide a continuous closed circuit but as the
current required to operate the bell buzzer or chimes is greater
than that to operate the bulb a slight movement in a bell is sometimes noticed but this is usually insignificant. The light from the
bulb goes out when the bell push is pressed because the push contacts short circuit the bulb to let the current flow through the push
contacts.

BELL TRANSFORMERS
The mains transformer supplying current to the bell circuit must
be of the double-wound type having an earthed secondary winding.
An auto-transformer which has a single winding may not be

used to supply a bell or other elv appliances. Proprietory bell transformers sold in the shops for the purpose are double-wound and meet the required regulations.

The transformer is supplied from the mains voltage wiring, the circuit and cable of which must be as for any other mains outlet or point. The cable, 1 sq. mm twin-core and earth pvc sheathed may be looped off a lighting circuit, either at a ceiling rose containing a live terminal as well as the necessary neutral, or it can be connected to a feed cable on the lighting circuit by inserting a joint box. Alternatively the transformer can be supplied from the ring circuit via a 3 amp fused connection unit. The mains cable is connected to the 240V input terminals of the transformer, the live conductor to one and the neutral conductor to the other. The earth continuity conductor is connected to the earth terminal of the transformer, or if all-insulated with no earth terminal it is connected to the centre terminal on the low voltage side of the transformer.

The three output or secondary terminals of the transformer give a choice of three voltages for the bell circuit. These are usually, 3V, 5V and 8V. The ratings are marked but the two outer terminals are always at the highest of the three voltage outputs. The 3V and the 5V tappings are used for bells or buzzers; the 8V tapping is used for door chimes. There are also bell trans-

Fig. 29   Mains and bell circuit connections to a transformer

Fig. 30   Bell circuit powered alternatively by battery and transformer

formers which provide other voltages, the most common being 4V, 8V and 12V. The 12V supply is required for some models of chimes, this being specified by the makers in the instructions supplied.

A bell or a buzzer can be operated from two push positions, such as at the front and back doors, but such an arrangement is only satisfactory using two bells with different notes on one bell and one buzzer. Two separate circuits are necessary, one for each, but both can be powered from the one battery or transformer because the likelihood of both pushes being operated simultaneously is remote.

Bell gongs are made in four types each giving a different tone. These are: round gong, the most commonplace of the four; sheep gong, the next in popularity; church gong used for special purposes; and wire gong which is a rare bell which produces an especially pleasing note. A front door single bell arrangement can be utilised to provide a second push station in say a bedroom or a sickroom, simply by running a twin bell wire from the push or the bell to the second push. By arranging a code, such as three rings for the sickroom interpretation of calls is possible.

EXTENSION BELLS
Where a second bell is required as an extension from the existing

single push at the front door there are three ways of arranging it. The two bells can be (i) wired in parallel; (ii) wired in series; (iii) operated in conjunction with a change-over switch so that either bell—not both—will ring according to where you want to hear it.

Parallel connection is not always satisfactory, because there is a tendency for one bell to deplete the current of the other. It is therefore necessary to step up the voltage of the supply either by adding more cells in series with the existing battery, or by using a higher voltage tapping on the transformer. But that is not the complete solution, for the bells must also have equal impedence:

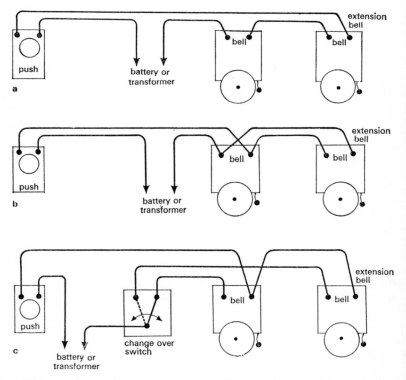

Fig. 31   (a) two bells wired in series (b) two bells wired in parallel
(c) two bells controlled by change-over switch

they must match and for this the wiring to the extension has to be taken into account. It is even more important that the bells are equally tuned by adjusting the contact setting screw. A more satisfactory arrangement can be made by connecting the bells in series but one must be modified. Two trembler bells, unless they are synchronised and remain so, will only ring intermittently, if at all. When the contacts of both bells are open no current will flow in the circuit. The second bell in the series must either be a single-stroke bell or it can be a trembler with the contacts shorted out so that it acts as a single stroke bell. As the trembler bell operates and alternates the current flow in the circuit, the single stroke bell also operates with a trembler action at the same frequency as the parent bell.

The most reliable arrangement is the change-over switch which allows only one bell to be operated at any one time. The only disadvantage here is that the switch must be manually operated each time the bell is needed at the extension position, and then switched back to the main bell. A change-over switch can be an ordinary 2-way light switch connected as in diagram 31c.

DOOR CHIMES

Door chimes are made in a variety of types and styles. Some have just a double note which emanates from one push—at the front door. Others provide both a double and a single note—the double note for the front door and the single note for the back door. Some use musical notes or church bell chimes. A few models are battery powered and some only work from a mains transformer. Others can be operated from either. The power source of some models is contained within the chime casing; for others the battery or transformer must be external.

The wiring circuit is the same as for a bell but the connection on the chimes vary with the model. The makers always supply a connection diagram so there is no problem.

FAULTS IN BELL CIRCUITS

When a bell, buzzer or chimes fail to operate, first check whether

H

the battery needs changing, or if transformer powered whether the circuit fuse has blown or the supply has been switched off— if locally switched at the outlet.

The most common fault occurs in the contact system and is usually rectified either by cleaning dirty contacts or by adjusting the contact screw. Two other faults can be that either the cover has fallen off the bell and fouled the striker arm, or that a circuit wire has broken (this is usually at a staple or where the wires are exposed to damage). A sticking plunger is a common fault on door chimes.

If the lamp of an illuminated push does not operate first check the circuit fuse and then take out and test the bulb. A dirty contact on the bell or a loose connection in the circuit will cause the bulb to go out.

15 | Domestic Electrical Appliances

Domestic electrical appliances are generally well designed and well made and can therefore be expected to give good service over many years, but they must be treated with care and be serviced periodically.

Many of the smaller servicing jobs can be undertaken by the householder but to attempt to overhaul the larger appliances termed in the trade 'white' appliances is inviting trouble. These which include refrigerators, freezers, washing machines, spin driers and also storage heaters should be serviced only by mechanics who have been trained for the job. Replacing a broken or worn component often means dismantling the appliance using special tools and equipment. Even the apparently simple job of replacing a belt on a spin drier or twin-tub machine may involve this which is beyond the knowledge and capability of the householder. Such servicing also requires a makers' manual which, unlike the motor car manual, is usually only available to authorised dealers and servicing firms.

To ensure that you can expect reasonably good service from your appliances you should buy only those made or distributed by reputable firms who have a good servicing organisation to carry out repairs. Most appliances sold in Britain carry a label which signifies they have been tested and approved electrically safe by the British Electrotechnical Approvals Board. Some appliances come within the BEAB scheme but do not carry labels. This does not mean that all appliances not approved, or that imported appliances are unsafe because there are a number of good reasons why some are not submitted for approval by the makers.

You should be careful about buying second-hand appliances and preferably buy only from firms you know to be reliable. Do not use an appliance you have picked up cheaply at a jumble sale until it has been properly tested. Don't give damaged or faulty appliances to a jumble sale. Those you send for scrap should be made beyond repair or they may be resold and result in an accident.

TYPES OF APPLIANCES

There are three principal types of domestic electrical appliance: (i) those with a heating element which include fires and cooking appliances; (ii) power-operated appliances such as vacuum cleaners and food mixers; and (iii) power-operated appliances which also have a heating element, such as hair driers and fan heaters.

GENERAL REPAIRS

When a portable appliance fails to work, first check the plug fuse. Remove the fuse from the plug and fit a known good one of the same current rating. Test the old one and if blown discard it immediately. If the fuse has not blown examine the flex for obvious signs of wear or damage. If both fuse and flex are all right it will be necessary to make a more detailed examination as outlined in the following pages. *Before you carry out any inspection or repairs to a portable appliance first remove the plug from its socket-outlet.*

REPAIRING ELECTRIC FIRES

The most common fault in an electric fire is a broken or loose element, or a broken or damaged flex.

Pencil rod elements of reflector fires are secured by: (i) milled nuts; (ii) fit into spring clips; or (iii) dagger type end caps which fit into spring loaded recessed contacts.

Loose contacts resulting in sparking is a common fault with the milled screw type but this can usually be rectified by tightening the milled nuts. Sparking between the rod terminal screw and the end of the element wire is also common, but easily cured by tightening the terminal screw.

A pencil rod element consists of a fireclay hollow rod with a straight wire element wound in a continuous groove. It is not practicable to rewind an element wire, so when it fails the complete rod has to be replaced. A break in the wire is either obvious, or has produced a blob of melted metal, or can be located by running a pencil along the coils. The element can be mains tested on the

centres

a

$\frac{9}{16}$" diameter
(14.287mm)

centres

pencil
rod elements

$\frac{9}{16}$" diameter
(14.287mm)

b

infra red tube elements—
adaptable for a wide range of appliances

total permissible
variation $1\frac{3}{4}$"

c

fire bar
element

d

Fig. 32 Various types of electric heater element

adjustable 2-pin

Edison screw fixing

Fig. 33   Two types of bowl fire element

bench using a pilot lamp but this has a high fire and shock risk
and should be left to the expert.

Pencil elements are made in a range of lengths and loadings
and with a variety of end caps. When replacing an element it
is essential for it to be the right length with the correct end caps.
Adjustable elements are available, giving a length variation of about
two inches, but are made in only the milled screw type. To
remove a pencil element it is necessary to remove the milled nut
or 'spring' the other type out of the clips, having first taken off
the dress guard in front of the heater.

A single-element portable electric radiant fire, including reflector types, have no built-in switch: the element is energised
when the power plug is inserted or the socket of the switched type,
switched on. This is a safety device to indicate when the flex and
heater are 'live'. A multi-element fire, without fuel effect, has
one non-switched element, but the remainder are usually individually switched. A fuel effect fire usually has all elements
individually switch-controlled because the imitation coal or logs or
other luminous device serves as the visual indicator.

As the non-switched element in multi-element fires is the one most frequently used this is the element most likely to fail first. You can delay the failure time by swopping elements occasionally. From the safety factor, it is important for the element of a single-element radiant fire and the non-switched element of a multi-element fire to be replaced as soon as they fail, even if this means 'robbing' one of the others. The lamp of a single-lamp fuel effect fire should be replaced without delay for the same reason.

Infra-red reflector fires
The elements of these fires are also of the rod type but are wire spirals enclosed in silica tubes. If the element has failed, but the tube is intact, you can fit a new spiral to the existing tube but it is far more satisfactory to buy a new element complete with silica tube and end contact caps.

The elements are made in a variety of lengths and in different loadings and with different types of end caps depending on the make and model of heater. It is therefore essential that you buy the correct replacement.

Fitting a new element
Remove the dress guard; release the screws holding the shields covering the ends of the element. Release the element from its fixture—this varies with the model. Insert the new element, replace the end shields and finally the dress guards.

Wall type infra-red reflector fires often have built-in cord-operated switches. If the cord breaks you can usually fit a new one to the existing switch, but if the switch fails you will need a new one.

Bowl fires
Bowl fires are reflector fires which have a spiral wire element fixed in grooves of a fireclay former, either cylindrical or spherical in shape. A new spiral can be wound on an existing former provided it is of the right length, and loading.

The complete element is secured to the fire assembly, by (i) plugging it in; (ii) screwing it into an Edison screw 'lamp-holder' or (iii) securing it with nuts and washers.

If the fireclay former is fractured the replacement must be identical. To rewind the former, remove the dress guard; release the complete element; carefully unwind the old spiral; measure its length; stretch out the new spiral about 3 in. short of the old one and wind it on securing and connecting it. Do not stretch it too much or it will sag when wound on the former causing coils of the spiral to 'short' and burn out the element. Replace the element and the dress guard.

Fire-bar radiant fires

The elements of this type of radiant fire are wire spirals fixed in grooves of a flat fireclay element (also known as brick type elements). These such as the Belling, Fig 32d, have five grooves. If the fireclay bar is intact you can fit a new spiral to the bar. The old spiral is removed by releasing the clips and disconnecting the ends of the terminals. Divide the new spiral into as many sections as there are grooves, one coil of the spiral at each end of each section being straightened to go round the ends of the grooves. The old fixing clips can usually be used again.

To remove a fire-bar element from the heater it is first necessary to take off the back panel by releasing nuts or screws, then you can disconnect the wires. These are usually stiff and uninsulated and remain in position to facilitate their re-connection. Now release the nuts or screws securing the fire bar and carefully lift it out.

When renewing elements polish the reflectors or wash them with soap and water so that they radiate the maximum heat. Also remove dust and foreign matter which will have collected in the body of a fire. Examine the flexible cord, especially the ends within the casing. Renew an old or worn flex making sure you know the connections for the new core colours.

Convector fires

Since the elements of convector fires operate at 'black' heat and

Left : instantaneous water heater (*Crownette*)   *Right :* storage water heater (*Santon*)

Extractor fan (*Philips*)

Fuel effect radiant heater (*Sunhouse*)

Convector heater (*Carniscot*)

Left : oil-filled radiator (*Hurseal*)   *Right :* washing machine, front loader (*Bendix*)

Fan heater (*Philips*)

Kettle (*Russell Hobbs*)

Food mixer (*Moulinex*)

therefore at comparatively low temperature they rarely fail or give trouble. When fitted with an illuminating device the lamp will need replacing but this is usually readily accessible. At the same time inspect the inside of the heater for foreign matter; convectors tend to draw in a lot of dust and fluff and this should be removed periodically. If the thermostat of a thermostatically controlled convector fails it will almost certainly have to be renewed and this is often a job for the expert.

Fan heaters, which are forced convectors, also need expert attention as the interior is complicated and hardly two models are identical.

Fuel effect heaters

Lamp failure is the most common fault. They are either the 2-pin type or have ordinary bc lamp caps. Access to a lamp is usually through the back panel of the fire and sometimes through the side or front. Replace a faulty lamp by one of the same type, wattage and colour. Take care how you remove the spinner or 'flicker' assembly for this is easily bent or misaligned. This and the collection of dust deposit are the principal reasons why spinners fail. Many modern electric fires have sophisticated fuel devices, some being motorised. Adjustment or repair of these is best left to the expert.

ELECTRIC IRONS

There are two principal types of electric iron: the standard iron, and the automatic thermostatically controlled iron in dry and steam versions. The standard iron is fitted with a removable flex connector which plugs into two pins behind the back of the handle. The metalwork is earthed by means of spring contacts on the flex connector which make a rubbing contact with the connector shield surrounding the pins on the body of the iron.

Common faults are: burnt out element; badly fitting flex connector; poor earth contacts; damaged or worn flex.

automatic electric iron

a   b

Fig. 34   (a) Flex connections of automatic iron (b) flex connector
of non-automatic iron

FITTING A NEW ELEMENT

Elements are made in a wide range of types and electrical loadings
and they are not interchangeable between different makes and
models of irons. It is usually wise to remove the old element first
to make sure that the new element is suitable. A universal element
is available and will fit a number of models for it has slots instead
of holes for the fixing studs.

Non-automatic iron

Remove the two domed nuts to release the handle; lift up the
metal cover plate and remove the terminal screws beneath the
contact pins to release the element contact strips. Remove the
two hexagonal nuts holding down the cast-iron pressure plate,
asbestos pad, and finally the element, which makes direct contact
with the sole plate and usually the source of the fault.

   Clean the sole plate surface using fine glass paper. Place the new
element in position and refit the asbestos pad and pressure plate

and finally the two hexagonal nuts. These nuts must be tightened as far as they will go to keep the element flat on the sole plate surface. Position the element contact strips so that they will not foul the pressure plate or cover plate and then connect them to the pin terminals. Finally replace the cover plate and handle, and secure them with the two domed nuts.

If the connector is in a poor condition replace it and fit a new 3-core unkinkable flex instead of the braided type you probably had originally on the iron.

Automatic electric iron
The flex of an automatic thermostatically controlled iron is connected direct to the terminals with no removable connector. It passes into the iron via a rubber or spring grommet and access to the terminals is obtained by removing a terminal cover, usually at the rear. The terminals are colour-coded to ensure that the thermostat is in the live pole.

Common faults in addition to element failure are: maladjustment of the thermostat which usually means the numbers of the dial do not correspond with the temperature of the sole plate and failure of the pilot light.

The thermostat is adjustable but this should not be attempted by the user: only a mechanic with the aid of the maker's servicing manual can do this. The householder can rarely do more than change the flex of an automatic iron. The element of some models is embedded in the sole plate and when it fails the complete sole plate must be renewed.

A steam iron is similar to the conventional automatic 'dry' iron from the repairs aspect. If tap water has been used instead of distilled water the vessel must be flushed out occasionally with a solution bought from an electrical shop or from the Electricity Board showrooms.

ELECTRIC KETTLES
Modern electric kettles have an immersion element which are easy to fit, but as there are numerous shapes and sizes and models

of kettles it is essential that you buy the correct replacement element when yours fails.

One variation in addition to shape and type is the diameter of the element flange hole in the kettle body. Two diameters: $1\frac{9}{16}$ in. (40 mm) and $1\frac{11}{16}$ in. (43 mm) fit the majority of standard or conventional-shape kettles, but it is usually best to ask first for the same type of element as originally supplied by the makers of your kettle. If this is not readily available you can buy a standard replacement element, pre-packed complete with element washers and with or without a new length of flex and connector. One element maker, Backer Electric Ltd, has introduced a special washer which enables a $1\frac{9}{16}$ in. element to be fitted into a $1\frac{11}{16}$ in. kettle orifice.

A 1kW or 1·5kW standard ordinary-speed kettle can be converted into a modern high-speed kettle with a pre-packed conversion kit containing a 2750 watt high-speed element, locking collar, 3-pin connector and a 4 ft length of 3-core kettle flex.

The latest innovation is the automatic kettle which switches itself off when boiling. This element can be fitted to many existing kettles and replaces the former safety device which ejected the flex connector and therefore switched off the current to the kettle as it boiled dry. In practice these ejectors do not always operate and have resulted in damage to kettle, connector and flex, and in some cases have resulted in serious fires. The thermostat of the new automatic device switches in again when the kettle has cooled down, and if the kettle is still left unattended it continues to cut in and out about four times each hour.

Replacing an element
Remove the connector and unscrew the collar or connector shield from the end of the element which secures it to the kettle. Remove the element by lifting it out through the kettle body. Scrape off the pieces of old washer around the flange hole, inside and outside the kettle. Fit the new rubber washer over the flange of the new element and put the element back into the kettle making sure it is the right way up. Fit the fibre washer on the

flange outside the kettle and screw on connector shroud or collar. Tighten the flange collar using a wrench if necessary but take care not to damage the chrome plating. When tightening, hold the element level in the kettle so that one edge is not in contact with the kettle base.

A new element usually requires a new flex connector, even where the existing one fits; but buy it with the element either separately or in a kit.

ELECTRIC TOASTERS

There are two types of toasters: the standard non-automatic, in which a slice of bread is toasted on one side and changed over by hand; and the automatic toaster.

Element and flex failure are the two most common faults which occur with the non-automatic toaster, plus mechanical faults such as a weak or broken spring of the toast retaining component. Elements are easily obtained for most models and are also easily fitted by removing two or more screws.

A common fault with the automatic toaster, apart from element burn-out, is the failure of the toast 'pop-up' mechanism. This device operates by means of a bi-metal strip or heat sensing device in conjunction with a solenoid which is a form of electro-magnet. The bread, usually two slices, is placed in the racks and passed into the toaster body by pressing a lever which loads a spring. The rack is locked in position and the elements are switched into circuit. The degree of browning required is selected by adjusting a control, and when the bread is toasted the heat sensing device unlocks and releases the spring and the toast 'pops-up'.

This is an intricate mechanism and must be serviced by the expert. It is unwise for the householder to attempt to replace a burnt-out element for this means dismantling the toaster which can upset the 'pop-up' mechanism.

ELECTRIC COOKERS

The free-standing family cooker is a comparatively simple piece of equipment though modern controls which provide automatic cooking have made it much more complicated. Apart from these controls, which are usually grouped on a panel, all the conventional cooker comprises is an oven, two or more hotplates and a grill. The oven is thermostatically controlled, and the hotplates and grill are controlled by variable switches. The hotplate elements, grill and oven are usually mineral insulated metal sheathed, have long life and rarely give trouble. Hotplates are made in a few standard diameters and are often interchangeable between makes. They are easily removed for replacement when they fail for they usually plug into sockets or are attached by a couple of screws. Grills too are made in various sizes and these plug into sockets. Like the hotplates they can be removed by lifting the hinged hob. Oven elements, usually one each side, also plug in and are removed by first taking out the vessel racks and side panels. An electric cooker can in fact be almost completely dismantled including the door which can be removed for periodic cleaning.

When an oven will not heat up or gets too hot the fault will usually lie in the thermostat, unless it is an automatic cooker and the controls have not been properly set or are inoperative. In either event, servicing is a job for the expert. The variable control of the hotplates and grill is a special unit operating on a thermo-time basis. A partial failure may mean an adjustment of the control by the expert but complete failure means a new control. Some grills and also some hotplates are controlled by 3-heat switches giving a choice of 'high', 'medium' and 'low' heat plus an 'off' position. The automatic controls, which include a clock and timer, should not be tampered with. It is, however, usually possible to replace a fluorescent tube in the panel, where fitted, but these have a long life and rarely need attention.

Table cookers

These cover a wide variety and range from a single hotplate to a 'baby' version of a free standing cooker. None have a loading in excess of 3kW and all are fitted with flexible cords which are plugged into the standard 13A (or 15A) socket-outlet.

Flex renewal and element replacement are the principal servicing jobs which can often be undertaken by the householder. The more complicated units should be left to the expert.

ELECTRIC BLANKETS AND BED-WARMERS

The electric blanket is among the most useful electrical 'appliances' in the home. They are made in a wide range of single- and double-bed sizes and types. The two principal types are under-blankets and over-blankets.

The over-blanket usually has a higher wattage loading and can be controlled by an automatic device which maintains it at a constant temperature even with a varying room temperature. Others have thermostats sewn into the blanket to switch off the current should a fault arise and produce a hot spot. The elements of some have a single wire operating in conjunction with the automatic controller to cut off the currents should a fault develop. This type of blanket is placed under the overlay, usually between other blankets, and may remain switched on all night even when the bed is occupied.

Most blankets operate at mains voltage but there is a range of low voltage blankets which operate through a mains transformer to eliminate any likelihood of electric shock. They are supplied from plug and socket-outlets which can be 13A socket-outlets with a 3A fused plug. It is *essential*, in the interests of safety, that electric blankets are fixed and used strictly in accordance with the makers' instructions; and that they are used with great care. *Never fix a blanket with any kind of pin!* Rucking or folding can damage the warming wires and lead to faults and possible fire. You should inspect a blanket and periodically return it to the makers for servicing every two years. If damaged or if water has been spilt on it—do not use it until it has been serviced.

Some thousands of fires arise each year from electric blankets and although this may be regarded as small in proportion to the millions of blankets in use, most could have been avoided if the blankets had been used or serviced correctly. Poor quality is also a cause of accidents but it is now an offence for a shop to sell an electric blanket which does not bear the BS Kite mark denoting its approved design and quality.

Bed-warmers

A bed-warmer is a metal-cased unit similar to an old-fashioned warming pan but with a short handle. It contains one or more electric light bulbs as the heat source. It is fairly low-priced, gives little or no trouble except for occasional lamp failure. It is used to pre-warm a bed as was the old-fashioned bed-warmer. One unit can serve one or more beds.

POWER-OPERATED DOMESTIC APPLIANCES

These appliances are those powered by an electric motor, and they cover a very wide range from clocks and shavers to refrigerators and freezers. The only difference between them and non-powered appliances, from the servicing aspect, is that they contain an electric motor. Otherwise, even flex replacement is the same. Some appliances require more attention than others depending on the type of electric motor.

There are two principal types of motor fitted to domestic appliances: the universal series wound commutator motor; and the induction motor.

The first type is the one likely to cause most trouble because it is fitted with carbon brushes. Appliances commonly used in the home powered this way are vacuum cleaners and polishers, electric drills or power tools as they are often termed, hair driers and hedge trimmers, sewing machines and mixers.

Induction motors are fitted to the larger appliances such as washing machines and refrigerators. These are very robust, have no brushes, and give no trouble over long periods which is often the lifetime of the appliance. There is, however, a small type of induction motor, termed a *shaded-pole motor*, which is fitted to extractor fans, fan heaters, small food mixers, some hair driers and numerous other small appliances including the motorised unit of fuel effect electric fires. It has no brushes, requires little or no attention throughout its lifetime and it has the advantage of being a variable-speed motor whereas the ordinary induction motor is only single-speed.

Commutator motors are also variable-speed machines and are used in conjunction with the electronic, thyrister, speed reducing control which is similar to the dimmer light switch.

Vacuum cleaners and floor polishers
The vacuum cleaner is among the most frequently used domestic appliance powered by a commutator motor. Electrical repairs which can be done by the householder are: fitting new brushes; fitting a new flex and attending to the switch. Belt renewal of the upright type of cleaner is also a periodic repair.

Of the two types of vacuum cleaner the upright one has more moving parts and requires most attention. The following is the sequence for fitting new brushes to the motor which should be done when the existing brushes are worn down to less than $\frac{3}{8}$ in.:

Buy correct replacement brushes.

Locate and remove brush caps.

Lift out old brushes and check that no particles are left in the brush holder.

Place new brush in each tube and check for ease of movement.

Slightly sandpaper a sticking brush.

Depress springs and re-fit the caps.

Brushes of polishers are similarly fitted.

When fitting new brushes to a cylinder type cleaner it is necessary first to remove the power unit. To do this you must take off the end cover from the cleaner.

Electric motors of vacuum cleaners sometimes burn out. This may be due to old age but is often because the moving parts of the cleaner become clogged with cottons, threads and other matter which stall or partially stalls the motor, overloads it and burns out the windings. Sometimes the armature (the rotating unit) burns out; sometimes the field coils (the stationary unit) burns out; sometimes both burn out. Replacement armatures and field coils can be bought on an exchange basis and fitted by the householder or the complete machine can be taken to a local

I

dealer. Premature failures can be prevented by keeping the cleaner free of dirt and emptying the dust bag each time the machine is used.

REFRIGERATORS AND DEEP FREEZERS

There are two types of refrigerator. One is the compressor type powered by an electric motor; the other is the absorption type which contains a small electric heating element.

Some versions of the absorption type refrigerator use a gas or oil heating element in which the heater evaporises the refrigerant. The compressor type evaporises the refrigerant by compressing it.

Refrigerators operate for many years without trouble if defrosted weekly (unless automatic). The motor and compressor of this type are contained in a sealed unit guaranteed for five years; any subsequent servicing must be done by a competent mechanic using special tools and gauges. The heating element of the absorption type is replaceable.

The advantage of the absorption refrigerator is that it is completely silent but the compressor type is cheaper to run, consuming less electricity per 24 hours*—but both are equally effective.

Deep freezers too have sealed units and should not be tampered with. They do not need de-frosting as a rule.

WASHING MACHINES AND SPIN DRIERS

Washing machines, spin driers and twin-tub machines cover a wide range of models. Some are fully automatic, some are semi-automatic, others are manual. The automatic and semi-automatic have intricate controls and must be serviced by the trained mechanic. Even replacing a belt on a spin drier can be complicated requiring partial dismantling of the machine and beyond the capabilities of the householder.

---

* *Author's note.* This no doubt appears contradictory, but the absorption type are in the smaller sizes only and are using current for longer times in a 24-hour cycle.

FOOD MIXERS

Both table and hand mixers have variable speeds and are usually powered by a shaded pole induction motor. These give little or no trouble when treated with reasonable care. Flexes should be examined periodically for signs of wear or damage and the brushes of commutator motors occasionally need attention. If a mixer appears to have lost some of its power the servicing agent should be consulted.

HAIR DRIERS

A hair drier operates on a similar principle to that of a fan heater: the motor drives a fan which passes air over an electric element which it expels through a nozzle. The heater cannot be switched into circuit until the fan is first switched on. If the motor fails to operate the heater will work but it is usually automatically switched off by a thermal cut-out before damage is caused to the appliance by excessive heat. The fan can be operated without the heater to provide cool air when required. The element is replaceable, and with some models this is easy to do by simply removing the nozzle and releasing the screws. Under no circumstances may a hair drier, or other portable mains appliance be used in the bathroom, unless a shaver from a socket incorporating a insulating transformer.

MAINS ELECTRIC CLOCKS

Apart from occasional oiling and possibly dusting the mains electric clock requires little attention. It has a conventional train of gears driven by a synchronous motor running at constant speed which is directly related to the speed of the generators at the power station. This enables power station engineers to keep clocks running at the right speed so they keep the correct time (provided the clock has been set at the right time when switched into circuit). Only during peak hours when power stations have had to shed some of their load by reducing the speed of the generators do clocks run slow. When the crisis is over the generators are speeded up to bring the clocks back to the correct time.

Therefore, when your clock runs slow because of load shedding you should not attempt to alter it but wait until the correct time is restored by the electricity authorities.

ELECTRIC SEWING MACHINES

Electric sewing machines cover a wide variety of models ranging from the conventional one powered by an electric motor, to highly sophisticated machines in which everything is done electrically. Hand-operated or a treadle foot-operated sewing machine can easily be converted by fitting a power unit.

Power units are available to fit almost every hand- or foot-operated model. A complete kit includes a foot controller to provide variable speeds during sewing, and can incorporate a light for easier threading. It is a commutator brush machine which requires the same attention as other appliances powered by this type of motor.

WASTE DISPOSERS

A waste disposer, which is a kind of mill, fitted beneath the sink waste outlet and plumbed to the waste pipe, pulverises remains of food and other kitchen refuse and washes it down the drain.

The sink waste hole has to be extra large ($3\frac{1}{2}$ in.) to accept the disposer. Some metal unit sinks $1\frac{1}{2}$ in. outlets can be enlarged to take the disposer connection but porcelain sinks cannot be modified. The waste disposer can be powered from a fused outlet, and can include controls which are fitted in a convenient position for the housewife.

EXTRACTOR FANS

The extractor fan is designed to expel stale and moist air from a room and to remove cooking smells from the kitchen. It is suitable for most rooms but especially so in the kitchen and bathroom where moisture causes condensation.

Fans are made in a range of types and sizes; the one most popular in the home is the type which fits in a hole cut in a pane of window glass. Sizes go by blade diameter which determines the rate of air extraction in a given period. Speed of fan is also important because the higher it is the more air extracted.

A suitable size for the average kitchen is 6 in. blade diameter with a speed of 6000–10,000 rpm but fans with blade diameters of 7 in. and 8 in. are also installed. Makers always specify the rate of air extraction and from this can be worked out the number of air changes per hour which the fan will provide, i.e. about twelve changes per hour in the kitchen: about twenty per hour in the bathroom. A window fan can be mounted in a hole cut in 32 oz. (40 mm) window glass and a glazier will cut this but at the customer's risk. Except for very large panes it is best to replace the existing pane with a new one which has the necessary hole cut by the glazier at the time of the purchase.

Positioning of the fan is important to get the maximum circulation of air. If fitted into a wall, there is a model designed for this, bear in mind that if a wind of more than 10 mph is blowing against that wall the fan's efficiency will be affected. Remember too that draught control of boilers can be affected by an extractor fan.

POWER TOOLS

The power tool and electric portable drill are operated by a universal series wound commutator motor of the same type as fitted to the vacuum cleaner, and many other high-speed domestic electrical appliances. The chuck containing the drill or other accessory is powered through a speed reduction gear box forming part of the power unit. Some models have a second, lower speed for heavy duty work. Speed variation below normal can be obtained from any portable power tool or drill by means of a transistorised electronic speed controller, inserted into the flexible cord usually at the plug end. These controllers, unlike resistance units, have the advantage of producing lower speeds without drop in torque.

Most causes of burn-out in the motor winding is overload, but the tool is easily dismantled and fitted with a replacement armature and/or field windings. The carbon brushes are also easily replaced. Periodic attention to the flexible cord is advised and the earthing connection should also be checked where relevant. Some models are double-insulated, require no earthing and are fitted with 2-core sheathed flex.

GARDEN TOOLS

The most commonly used electric garden tool is the hedge trimmer powered by a commutator brush motor similar to that of the portable drill, and requiring similar servicing. Double-insulated versions are preferable from the safety angle, though one tool maker supplies a flexible lead incorporating a high sensitivity earth leakage circuit breaker which trips if the sheath is damaged before the live conductor is cut, or comes into contact with the live conductor of the flex.

Additional safety is provided with another model which operates at reduced voltage through a portable mains transformer.

ELECTRIC MOWERS

For the larger lawn a battery powered mower is well worth while but the battery has to be charged at the end of a short mowing session. Most low-priced mowers operating from the mains are the rotary type with the blade powered by a commutator motor. These have a thermal cut-out to reduce a likelihood of the motor burning out should the blade become obstructed in long grass or fouled by rubbish or undergrowth. The units are mainly double-insulated and are therefore fitted with 2-core sheathed flex.

Electric cylinder-type mowers in the higher price range are powered by induction motors which drive the cylinder by a belt and pulleys. Some also propel the mower, as do engine driven machines.

When using either a hedge trimmer or mower there is always the risk of cutting the flex. With the hedge trimmer, this can be avoided by throwing the flex over the left shoulder; with the mower you should lay the flex out of the run of the machine. An additional hazard, particularly with the rotary mower, is running over pebbles hidden in the long grass. These not only damage the cutting blade but are ejected from under the mower at a great force and can result in personal injury. The grass should be swept prior to mowing to prevent this.

TABLE 6

Appliance	Loading Watts
Bed warmer	60–100W
Blankets	50–150W
Boiling ring	750–2000W
Bottle warmer	150–180W
Car heater	300–500W
Clocks	negligible
Coffee maker	380–1200W
Coffee percolator	400–800W
Dish washer	3000W (with heater)
Fans	25–120W
Fires	
1, 2, and 3-bar	1000–3000W
infra-red	750–2250W
bowl	500–750W
Floor polisher	300–450W
Food mixer	100–450W
Food trolley (hostess)	200–450W
Frypan	1000–1250W
Hair drier	350–600W
Infra-red grill	1500–3000W
Iron, automatic,	750–1000W
standard type	450–500W
Jug	600W
Kettle	1000–3000W
Plate warmer	175–800W
Power-operated tools	210–260W
Radio receiver	100W
Refrigerators	
absorption type	80–115W
compressor type	100–175W
home freezers	100–250W

TABLE 6 *cont.*

Appliance	Loading Watts
Scrubbers and polishers (combined)	300–450W
Sewing machines	75W
Shaver	15W
Spin drier	100–320W
Spit (rotary)	650–2000W
Tea maker	500–750W
Television receiver	100–200W
Toaster	400–600W
Tumbler drier	2500–2750W
Urn	3000W
Vacuum cleaner	220–300W
hand cleaner type	150W
Washboiler	3000W
Washing machine (unheated)	300W
Washing machine (heated)	3000W
Waste disposer	200W

16 | Festive Lighting

Coloured lamps for the Christmas tree may only be used indoors. They are wired in series and are low voltage, but because they are connected to the mains supply they can give a severe shock if an exposed metal cap or filament of a broken lamp are touched by someone in the vicinity of earthed metal or a stone floor.

The voltage of each lamp depends on how many there are in a festoon. Those in a 12-lamp festoon are 20V, in a 20-lamp festoon 12V, and in a 40-lamp festoon, 6V lamps. It is therefore essential to replace a lamp by one of the correct voltage: this is stamped on the lamp cap.

There are two principal types of indoor festoons. One has olive or similar shape lamps or large torch-type bulbs inside decorative figures; all have mes (miniature Edison screw) lamp caps, like torches. The other type has small 'pinhead' lamps with a tiny les (lilliput Edison screw) screw cap originally of Continental design. These are in 20- and 40-lamp festoons.

As they are wired in series, when one lamp is missing none works. When the mes type fails, one dud lamp puts the whole festoon out of action until it is replaced. When a 'pinhead' type of lamp fails, a shorting device in it maintains the current in the circuit and all the rest remain alight. But this means that the same mains voltage is now applied to fewer lamps in the series, so the voltage at each becomes higher and the lamps are 'over-run'. Other lamps consequently fail and within a short period the whole string will fail. To avoid this chain reaction it is essential to replace a 'pinhead' lamp immediately it goes out.

When a conventional mes lamp fails and the whole festoon goes out it is difficult to locate the dud, especially on a Christmas tree amongst the other decorations and presents. One method is to replace each lamp in turn with a new one, first making sure that each lamp is secure and making contact in its lampholder. A better method is to test each lamp in turn with a 6-volt battery.

Lamp life can be increased by inserting a mains voltage coloured lamp into the festoon, or increased almost indefinitely by connecting two identical festoons in series. The lamps will lose some of their sparkle but will be more reliable.

Some festoons include a flasher lamp, if not one can be wired into the circuit unless they interfere with TV or radio reception.

The total load (wattage) of a festoon is much higher than generally realised and it can easily overload a lighting circuit. It is better therefore to supply them from 13A ring circuit plugs and sockets with 3A fuses fitted to the plugs.

OUTDOOR DECORATIONS
Festoons made especially for outdoor use are weatherproof. The lamps are mains operated coloured bulbs, either of conventional shape or they are 'specials'.

Lampholders are moulded into the plastic sheath of the cable to exclude moisture. There is also a press-pin type which is fitted to rubber sheathed twin-core cable. When the two sections of the lampholder are secured together on the cable the pins make contact with the stranded conductors of the cable. These festoons are widely used in municipal illumination schemes, but in the home they must be used with care and the lampholders, once fixed, should remain in the one position. Should a lampholder be removed, moisture and rain may penetrate the pin holes through to the conductor and result in current leakage and possible shock.

Outdoor festoons can be run off garden socket-outlets or from the house using circular pvc sheathed flexible cord.

17 | Safety in Home Electrics

Correct wiring, high quality appliances and their careful use with regular servicing are important factors for safety in home electrics. This applies to the whole installation but there are special situations where extra precautions are necessary. One is in the bathroom. The requirements here are as follows:

1. No socket-outlet may be installed in the bathroom or any room containing a fixed bath or shower. No mains operated portable electrical appliance may be taken into or used in the bathroom, with one exception, an electric shaver operated from a shaver supply unit to British Standard BS.3052.

This type of socket unit contains a double-pole isolating transformer, plus a thermal cut-out to prevent any appliance other than the low-voltage shaver being plugged into it. The supply at the socket is at mains voltage, but it is isolated from the earthed mains to prevent shock to a person using the shaver who might touch an exposed contact when he is in contact with earthed metal.

2. No switch must be fixed within reach of someone using the bath or shower, except the insulated cord of a cord-operated ceiling switch. The alternative to a ceiling switch is one fixed on the wall immediately outside the bathroom door.

3. A light fitting in the bathroom should be totally enclosed. If an open lampholder, such as a batten lampholder, is fixed to the ceiling it must have a HO (Home Office) skirt to shield the metal cap of the bulb so that it cannot be touched when it is being taken out. A flexible cord pendant should not be installed in the bathroom.

4. A shaving mirror light, usually a striplight, must be the type which has metal lamp caps that cannot be touched even when replacing the lamp. Mirror lighting units containing a shaver

socket must be designed especially for bathroom use, with the shaver socket supplied from a double-wound transformer complying with BS.3052. The light switch, unless cord operated, must be out of reach of a person using the bath, and it should be operated by a cord switch.

5. Where the hot water tank cupboard opens on to the bathroom the immersion heater must not be supplied from a plug and socket but from a switch placed well out of reach.

6. Exposed metalwork in the bathroom should be bonded (see Bonding).

OTHER SAFETY PRECAUTIONS

As detailed in this book elsewhere, electrical appliances must be kept in good order and used properly. Wiring and accessories which become loose or damaged must be attended to without delay. Correct fuses must be used to replace blown ones and the fault which caused the fuse to blow must be located and rectified.

One very important safety factor is to unplug portable appliances when they are not being used. This particularly applies to radiant electric fires which might be placed up against furniture or other inflammable material which, if the plug was inadvertently switched on, would result in a very serious fire. And to power operated appliances especially food mixers, which if left on the kitchen table or work area would be a danger to young children. If the power tool, hedge trimmer or mower is left unattended for a while, *pull out the plug*. Also, where there are young children, make a habit of turning off the cooker control switch when you are not using it. This will stop the clock, if one is fitted, but it will also prevent accidents where children can meddle with low-level switches.

If you change from a standard kettle to a high-speed one stay beside it during the few minutes it takes to boil. No doubt the automatic device will operate but there is no point in leaving a kettle to boil dry while you answer the door or are engaged on the 'phone.

SOME SAFETY *DONT'S*

Don't patch up frayed flex with insulation tape but renew it at the first sign of wear or damage.

Don't run flex under carpets.

Don't use twin-twisted type flex for appliances.

Don't drag a vacuum cleaner or any appliance along by its flex.

Don't connect 3-core flex to a 2-pin plug.

Don't use 2-core flex for appliances except those of the double insulated type marked with a double square.

Don't let flex droop over a radiant fire or over a cooker hotplate.

Don't wrap the flex around an iron while the iron is still hot.

Don't plug a number of appliances into a socket-outlet by means of multi-plug adaptors. Apart from a risk of overloading the socket this practice usually means long trailing flexes.

Don't have unnecessarily long flexes; keep them as short as possible.

Don't have too short a flex on an iron or kettle where this would place undue strain on the flex and may prevent the appliance being used with safety.

Don't connect more than one flex to a ceiling rose designed to take only one.

Don't run an appliance from a light fitting using a lampholder adaptor.

Don't renew a bulb without first switching off the light.

Don't stand a radiant electric fire against furniture or fabric, or face it against the wall or woodwork.

Don't stand a storage heater right against a wall unless the heater is of the recessed type.

Don't place clothes or materials to dry or air over a convector heater, over a fan heater or over the outlet grille of a storage fan heater.

Don't let materials fall on to tubular heaters or let curtains come in contact with the tubes.

Don't have an airing cupboard heater at low level without a clothes guard.

Don't touch the element of an electric fire without first pulling out the plug or turning off the main switch, if of the built-in type not supplied from a plug and socket.

Don't dismantle a cooker for cleaning without first turning off the control switch.

Don't let cooking metal foil come into contact with elements of the open spiral wire type.

Don't use the blade of a knife or other metal object to remove bits of broken bread from a toaster, and also always first pull out the plug before attempting to clean it.

Don't use an inspection light at mains voltage when working on, or under, the car unless it's an all-insulated type of lamp with the bulb well guarded from touch should the glass break.

Don't knock nails into walls, or use drills or plugging tools to drill holes, in walls immediately above switches and socket outlets or where you suspect electric cables are buried.

Don't knock nails into floorboards which are likely to have electric cables underneath them.

18 | Inspecting and Testing an Installation

The home installation should be inspected and tested periodically. This is carried out by the Electricity Board prior to the connection of an installation or of an extension, but it is often the only test made until the Board is called in again to add further wiring to the supply.

The Institution of Electrical Engineers recommends that tests should be made after the first five years, and subsequent ones at shorter intervals. But this is rarely done for the initiative lies with the householder. Since there are over 17 million dwellings in Britain it would be a colossal task to carry out tests frequently. An electrical contractor or the Board makes a charge for such tests.

WHAT THE HOUSEHOLDER CAN DO

The householder can inspect the wiring but without the necessary instruments he is unable to make the same tests as the contractor or Electricity Board.

A test is made up of four parts:
   (i) Verification of polarity.
  (ii) Earthing effectiveness.
 (iii) Insulation resistance test.
 (iv) Ring circuit continuity.

Verification of Polarity

Every light switch and most other switches, except that of the mains, is single-pole. This means that when they are switched off the switch breaks the current in the circuit at one of the two conductors.

Since one of the two poles of a circuit is the 'live' pole and the other is the neutral, but at earth potential, it is essential for the single-pole switch to break the current in the live pole; and not in the neutral.

Should the switch be inserted in the neutral pole, turning it off would cut off the flow of current but the terminals at a light fitting or appliance would still be live.

For example one of the pins of a lampholder would remain 'live' with the wall switch turned off. A person replacing a lamp thinking the current is off might touch the live pin and if in contact with the earth or earthed metal would receive a severe electric shock.

A simple test for this can be made by inserting the blade of a neon screwdriver into the lampholder, but in view of the shock risk great care is necessary.

Where mains voltage es (Edison screw) bulbs and lampholders are fitted it is essential that the centre contact of each es lampholder is connected to the 'live' pole.

Correct polarity is also important with socket-outlets. This ensures that the fuse of a plug is in the 'live' pole and that appliance single-pole switches and thermostats (also single-pole) break the 'live' pole. If the socket-outlet, or the plug flex is incorrectly connected, the appliance switch or thermostat will not be in the 'live' pole.

The polarity of a socket-outlet can be tested with a special testing plug which has a neon indicator.

When testing the lighting circuit, if all or most of the switches are in the neutral pole it is fairly obvious that the circuit conductors have been incorrectly connected at the fuse board or consumer unit and need changing over. If only one or perhaps two lighting switches are wrong the fault can be traced to a joint box or to a loop-in ceiling rose. To remedy it, find out which joint box or ceiling rose and change the two conductors over. The colour coding of circuit cable conductors is red for the 'live' and black for the neutral, but as a sheathed cable often uses black as the switch wire (which is on the live side of the circuit) the code is not an infallible guide. Where black insulated cable is used for the 'live' place red adhesive tape on the ends for identification.

The same rule can apply to socket-outlets—if all or most have reverse polarity the connections at the fuseway are reversed, but if only the odd one or so is wrong the conductors at the socket are reversed. With these circuits the colour code can be followed. *Black must be connected to black, and red to red throughout.*

TESTS FOR EARTHING EFFECTIVENESS

I have already stressed the importance of earthing in another chapter. Not only must it be continuous throughout all circuits but the earth current path—the earth loop—back to the Electricity Board's sub-station must be of low impedance to carry adequate fault current to blow the fuse when a fault develops. The test for this is made with an earth loop impedance tester which plugs into a live socket-outlet of the installation and sends a current of about 25 amps through the loop. If the impedance from one socket is all right then that for the whole installation will be satisfactory. It is also necessary to check the ecc resistance of all the circuits and preferably at every socket and switch position but to do this requires an ohmmeter—not normally available to the householder.

The householder should make a regular physical examination of the earthing to check the following points: that the earthing clamp is securely fixed; that there are no signs of corrosion on the terminal; that the earth core of flexible cords is connected to the earth terminal of plugs, and to the earth terminal in appliances.

It is also possible to check the continuity of the whole earth loop using live current from the mains. A test lamp is connected by twin flex to the live and earth terminal of a plug, and the plug inserted into each socket in turn. If the earth is continuous the lamp will light at full strength.

This test only checks the continuity of the earthing. It does not check its effectiveness for carrying heavy fault currents for which a proper instrument tester is required.

K

INSULATION RESISTANCE TEST

This test is to check that the insulation of conductors is good, and that there will be no current leakage between conductors of different polarity or between a conductor and earth. It can only be made with an insulation resistance tester. The resistance should be not less than 1 megohm but it will normally be at, or near, infinity. If there is a fault such as a short circuit, or an earth fault 'of negligible impedance' caused by say a nail through the cable, or maybe a wrong connection, the installation tester will indicate the fault but not where it is. Locating a fault is more difficult, and is a job for the expert.

TEST OF RING CIRCUIT CONTINUITY

As shown in Chapter 12 the cable of a ring circuit must be wired in to form a ring starting and ending at the terminals of a 30A fuseway in the consumer unit. When socket and other fused outlets and joint boxes are inserted into the ring cable, the connections must be properly made to the terminals of the accessories so that the electrical circuit is complete throughout the ring.

At each outlet or joint box there is an incoming and outgoing cable see Fig. 25.

The continuity test checks that outlets are connected to the ring cable and not to spurs branching off it and that the ring extends throughout a substantial part of the area covered by the sockets on the ring and spurs.

A continuity test can be made at the fuseway by means of an installation tester applied across the ends of the two cables—outgoings and incoming—but only a physical check at various sockets and fused outlets will show which are connected to the ring cable and which are fed from spurs.

The householder can make a physical check by removing sockets from their boxes but without a tester the job is complicated, except with outlets supplied from one cable only which are obviously spur sockets. A socket-outlet having two cables may be a ring cable socket or the first rocket of a two socket-outlet spur.

WHAT THE BOARD INSPECTOR LOOKS FOR

If a new installation wired by a contractor does not pass the Electricity Board's test, then it is the contractor not the householder who is responsible. In practice the contractor will make a test and if he is registered the Board will accept his certificate without making a further test.

Where the householder has done the wiring it should not fail the test if the information in this book is followed and competently carried out.

When the Board inspector examines and tests a new installation or an extension to an existing one, prior to connecting it to the mains, he has to be satisfied that the wiring and equipment is safe and that it will not interfere with other consumers' supply. He expects the installation to comply with IEE Wiring Regulations (the Regulations for the Electrical Equipment of Buildings).

If it does the Board is bound by statute to connect it, or the parts that do, if such a division is practicable. If the installation does not comply with the regulations in every respect the Board has no statutory powers to withhold a connection solely on those grounds. He must show that the installation would be dangerous or would interfere with the supply to others.

Refusal to connect usually means that something is seriously wrong and not just that fixing clips of cables are too widely spaced or similar minor items do not comply. The initial test is free of charge but a charge is made for subsequent visits.

Tests made are for the four points outlined above, and how extensive these are depends, partly, on the individual inspector for his findings benefit the Board and not the consumer. Although a consumer does gain from the knowledge that the Board has accepted the installation, he cannot regard it as a guarantee of good workmanship or hold the Board responsible if something later proves to be wrong or faulty.

Likely interference with the supply to others applies mainly to equipment; in particular to electric motors, fluorescent fittings and other inductive apparatus. Electric motors of the larger sizes are rarely installed in the home but it is one class of apparatus where interference can be expected. The choke of fluorescent fittings is highly inductive and with most circuits causes a poor power factor which consumes wattless current not registered on the meter. A power factor correction capacitor has to be included in the circuit, but is fitted by the manufacturer and is necessary in home-constructed units built from kits of components.

WHEN A RE-WIRE BECOMES NECESSARY

An installation wired before the last war, and some in the early post-war years, employed rubber insulated and rubber sheathed cable. The rubber has a limited life, not much more than 25–30 years, which means that most installations need re-wiring now (where the cable has not been disturbed a longer life can be expected). Experience shows that most installations have, to some extent, been disturbed if only to replace light fittings.

Pvc insulation, on the other hand, does not deteriorate with age and as most installations are now wired in pvc insulated and sheathed cable provision for re-wiring is no longer considered necessary.

The older installation

The most obvious sign of age in rubber insulated cables is that the insulation has become hard and brittle and when handled falls off the conductor leaving it bare. This is specially so at the ends of sheathed conductors where the sheath was removed for making the connection to the switch or ceiling rose. Both the vri (vulcanised rubber insulation), and the sheath of trs (tough rubber sheath) cables are highly combustible and will start a fire where the conductor joints are poor and sparking occurs.

Cables enclosed in conduit, usually metal in the older installation, also have vri insulation but this is wrapped in tape and covered in braid (red for the live and black for the neutral). This too is highly combustible. Conduits should terminate in metal boxes at the ceiling rose and at switches and other outlets so that the vri cables are completely enclosed in incombustible material.

In the older installation conduits usually terminate a few inches from the outlet leaving the conductors exposed and a fire risk.

Switches and accessories
The older switch, ceiling rose, light fitting, socket-outlet and other accessories usually mounted on wood blocks are now obsolete. They should be replaced by modern switches and accessories, mounted on plastic surface boxes or metal flush boxes with the sheath of the cable passing into the box. Modern ceiling rose and ceiling switches are mainly enclosed and require no mounting box.

Main switches and fuses
Where the older installation has a number of main switch and fuse units for the various circuits, instead of one composite consumer unit for all, they should be given early attention but to replace them will involve some re-wiring. Those which have double-pole fuses should be replaced by single-pole fuse units without delay. Earthing of metal lighting fittings and switches is also an urgent job. Any 2-pin plugs and socket-outlets, other than the modern shaver socket, should be replaced by 3-pin versions and an earth continuity conductor run to each one.

THE MODERN INSTALLATION
The modern installation is usually wired in non-combustible pvc sheathed cable. Where wires are in high ambient temperatures, such as at the ends where they terminate in enclosed light fittings and where there is heat transferred from the lamp to the conductors, via the lampholder, the pvc is liable to melt and cause corrosion of the copper conductors. Ends of the cables where this is likely to happen should be examined and the final few inches replaced by heat resistant cable with silicon rubber insulation. To effect the conversion, a joint box or special pattress box fitted with terminals is needed.

Earthing of metal light fittings and switches is also important because only the more recently wired lighting circuit will have cables embodying an earth continuity conductor.

All circuits should be checked for possible overload, especially where points have been added since the installation was first wired. Finally, any loose switches, light fittings, socket-outlets and other accessories must be securely fixed even though this may mean removing the fitting to provide better support or re-plugging the wall to secure the pattress box. Damaged or broken accessories must be replaced without delay.

BEWARE OF MOONLIGHTERS

Because re-wiring has become a priority job in the older, owner-occupier dwelling householders in some districts are pestered by people offering to do this job at seemingly attractive prices. These self-appointed electricians are mainly unqualified and employed in other jobs during the day. Some offer a free inspection with the intention of frightening the householder into having work done whether necessary or not, as proved in one case where the property had only been rewired a couple of years earlier.

The prices quoted are for the bare minimum which, with the necessary 'extras', brings the final price to an exorbitant figure and does not include making good chases in plaster or re-laying floor coverings. The Electricity Board or a reputable contractor will make a test for a reasonable figure, and it is best to get quotations from the Board and from two registered contractors whose names can be obtained from the Board's offices.

These jobs carry a guarantee and extended payment terms can be arranged, but unless part of other improvements the work does not qualify for a government home improvement grant.

19 | Getting a Supply of Electricity

When you move house it is necessary to apply to the local Electricity Board for a supply of electricity. You can write to them, or if in the neighbourhood you can call at their showrooms.

You will receive an application form for you to give details of when you want the supply to commence, and where the Board official can get the key if you have not already moved into the premises. Details of the appliances and lamps and any special equipment including fluorescent lights which you will have connected will also have to be supplied. This information enables the Board to check that the service cable is adequate for the assumed current demand and the current rating of the meter.

If wiring work has been carried out since the last occupier vacated the premises you, or your contractor if you have employed one, will have to give details on the relevant form.

If the house has been occupied very recently the connection of the meter will be little more than a 'matter of form', and may involve no more than replacing the Board's service fuse by an official. If you move in the same day or the day after the previous occupier moves out, possibly only the meter will be read without the need for temporary disconnection.

Either way the Board inspector may wish to test and inspect the installation for his own satisfaction. If it does not come up to the required standard or does not comply with the regulations the Board is unlikely to disconnect or refuse to re-connect it—their powers are limited by statute to situations which are specifically dangerous. The usual procedure is to make a 'temporary connection' which is followed by a letter detailing what is wrong and requesting that the 'faults' are rectified. (See Inspecting and Testing an Installation.) If the house is a new one and you the first occupier, testing the installation will be the responsibility of the builder's electrician and should there be anything wrong he will have to put it right, but not at your expense.

SERVICE CHARGES

If you move into a house or cottage without a mains supply of electricity, and you intend having the supply to the premises you will probably be asked by the Board to make a contribution towards the cost in the form of a service charge. The amount will depend upon the distance of the premises from the distribution cable and the position of the meter in the house.

If the distribution cable does not run along the street or lane, or if it is an overhead cable more than about 60 ft (20 m) away, the contribution you have to make can be quite high. The Board does not expect the whole cost of the service to be met by the consumer, and is usually prepared to negotiate when load such as cooking and storage heating is installed which provides substantial revenue. If only lighting is required the contribution is likely to be higher. Where more than one house requires a supply, much of the cost can be shared and individual contributions made smaller.

20 Paying for your Electricity

An electricity tariff is the means of charging for electricity consumed by the particular service provided. Each area Electricity Board has a number of different tariffs and the consumer has a choice. They operate on a quarterly basis and generally the more units consumed the cheaper the average price per unit of the electricity used.

The most widely adopted domestic rate is the block tariff. With this the first block of 50–90 units consumed each quarter are charged for at a fairly high rate and all subsequent units used during the same period are cheaper. The higher initial cost is to pay for providing the service including the meter for which a rental used to be charged. The actual number of units at the higher rate varies with each Electricity Board as does the price per unit: more units in the first block usually means a lower price per unit.

For example: in the Midlands Board area the first block of 52 units per quarter are charged at 3·5p per unit; in the North Eastern Board area the first block of 78 units are charged at 3p per unit; and in the North of Scotland area the first block of 90 units are charged at 2·85p per unit. Some Boards have an intermediate block of units in a 3-block tariff and charge a little over 1p per unit for about 70 units per quarter, but all Boards with a domestic block tariff whether of 2- or 3-blocks charge 0·8–0·9p per unit for all remaining units consumed during the quarter.

In these three examples the cost of the first blocks work out at £1·82; £2·240; and £2·565 per quarter respectively. This represents a fixed charge for the service plus the cost of supplying the units consumed.

Three Electricity Boards have no domestic block tariff but instead have a two-part tariff consisting of a fixed quarterly charge plus a flat rate of about 0·9p per unit for all electricity consumed. Where only a very small amount of electricity is used the Board charges less and averages out the unit charge at not more than the statutory maximum. This takes the place of the normal flat-rate tariff. Where a prepayment meter (slot meter) is installed a surcharge is added to each unit to pay for the collection of coins and other costs.

THE WHITE METER TARIFF

Every Electricity Board has a domestic time of day tariff, known as the 'White Meter' tariff because the necessary 2-rate meter is in a white case. This is an alternative to the block rate—or two-part tariff in those areas where there is no domestic block rate.

This tariff consists of a quarterly fixed charge plus a unit charge for electricity consumed. The unit charge itself is in two parts: a day rate at about 0·9p per unit and a night rate at about half the price. The night rate usually covers an eight-hour period and starts at 11 p.m., ending at 7 o'clock the following morning. Times vary slightly between Boards and with one, the Eastern Board, it lasts ten hours and starts at 9 p.m. In addition, there is a fixed charge—from about £2·50 to £3.50 per quarter according to the Board area. This charge includes a rental for the meter and necessary time-switch for the change of rate.

Generally the day rate on the White Meter tariff is slightly more than that of the block tariff or two-part tariff, but is compensated by the fact that all services, including lighting used during the overnight period, is charged at the lower rate. It replaces the former off-peak tariff which was exclusively for storage heating and storage water heating including immersion heaters. Conventional off-peak tariffs are still available in some Board areas but have limited application.

NB. *All tariff prices shown are subject to change but the basic structure remains.*

WHICH TARIFF TO CHOOSE

When you move house it is necessary to decide which tariff you intend to adopt. Unless you have electric storage heating, you will usually find that the block tariff or two-part tariff of most financial benefit. If you do not have night storage heating the Electricity Board representative will no doubt advise against the White Meter tariff unless you expect to use an abnormally large amount of electricity during the cheap-rate period. You have to allow for the fixed charge and the increase in the day rate on the White Meter tariff before you can expect an advantage.

You can change to White Meter tariff at any time, but as it must run for at least a year you cannot have the advantage of it in the winter and then discard it in the summer when you are not likely to use so much electricity at night.

When you have the White Meter tariff you can check the consumption of the two rates by referring to the figures on your electricity bills over the year, but don't forget to add the fixed charge.

WHAT TO DO ABOUT AN EXTRA-HIGH BILL

When you receive what appears to be an excessive bill for the quarter's electricity, the most likely answer is that you have in fact used the amount of electricity indicated. Try to recall whether fires were left on for exceptionally long periods during a cold spell or during an illness, or that an immersion heater was left switched on by mistake.

Another possible reason is that previous bills were based on estimated consumption, because you were out when the meter reader called, and low estimates have now caught up with you following an actual meter reading. If you make a check of the meter reading after the amount has been estimated you will know whether a substantial bill is being 'clocked up'.

If there is no obvious solution you can consult the Board for there may be an accounting mistake.

As a final resort you can question the accuracy of the meter and possibly have a check meter installed for a period. If you are not genuinely satisfied you have the right to have the meter tested at an official testing station which comes under the jurisdiction of the Department of Industry. If this shows the meter to be accurate you will have to pay for the test. If it is inaccurate there is no charge and your bill will be adjusted, but remember the test may show that the meter is reading slow, not fast, and any adjustment of your bill might not be in your favour. Rarely is a meter found to be reading high or inaccurate for each one is tested as a statutory requirement.

To query an account does not give a consumer any rights to withhold payment for this could also be used as an excuse to delay payment of the account due.

Every householder should learn to read a meter. The White Meter has digital dials which are as easy to read as the mileage on a car odometer. Meters with clock dials require experience and are not easy to read unless you know how.

For practice study the dial in Fig. 35. Ignore the small dial on the extreme right marked $\frac{1}{10}$ kWh and read the others from left to right. Where a pointer is at a whole number and it is difficult to tell whether it has reached or passed it, check the next lower

Fig. 35　Reading an electricity meter

dial on the right. If the pointer of that one is between the 9 and 0 you take the lower number of the dial in question. If the pointer of the dial on the right is between the 0 and 1 you take the higher number. For example, the pointer on the first dial in Fig. 35 is at the 3 but as the pointer on the next dial is between 9 and 0 the figure to read is 2, which is a difference of 1000kWh (units). Where the pointer is between two numbers, as is usual, the correct reading is always the lower number. The meter in the Fig. 35 reads 2978kWh

Index

Compiled by Gordon Robinson

Asterisks indicate an illustration